# The Church
## God's Called Out People

By Matthew Allen

© 2022 Spiritbuilding Publishers.
All rights reserved. No part of this book may be reproduced in any form without the written permission of the publisher.

Published by
Spiritbuilding Publishers
9700 Ferry Road, Waynesville, Ohio 45068

THE CHURCH
God's Called Out People
by Matthew Allen

ISBN: 978-1955285-49-0

All Scripture references are taken from Holman Bible Publishers' *Christian Standard Bible* unless otherwise noted.

# Spiritbuilding
PUBLISHERS

spiritbuilding.com

# Table of Contents

Why This Study? .................................................. 1

**Lesson 1**    Your Story Is His Story ........................................ 2

**Lesson 2**    The Magnitude of Your Salvation ........................... 8

**Lesson 3**    Defining New Testament Christianity ..................... 15

**Lesson 4**    Identifying the New Testament Church ..................... 23

**Lesson 5**    How to Be Added to the Church ........................... 31

**Lesson 6**    The Role of Jesus and the Apostles in the Church ............ 42

**Lesson 7**    The Eldership ................................................ 50

**Lesson 8**    Deacons and Evangelists .................................... 58

**Lesson 9**    The Heart Behind Giving .................................... 64

**Lesson 10**    The Work of the Lord's People .............................. 71

**Lesson 11**    The Reverence of Worship .................................. 78

**Lesson 12**    The Purpose and Power of the Lord's Supper ............... 83

**Lesson 13**    Why We Sing A Cappella .................................... 89

## Why This Study?

- To realize just how precious the church is
- To understand we are part of something bigger than ourselves
- To understand God's purpose for you in the church
- To know what the future holds for the church

# Lesson 1

# Your Story Is His Story

## The Greatest Story Ever Told

What's your story?

How did you get to here, to this exact moment?

Stories have a unique power.[1] They capture us and enthrall us in ways that facts, information, and systems can't. A story organizes events into a sequence that can be followed and understood. Stories often contain morals and lessons that teach us about universal truths of life. They help us to make sense of reality and confront the chaos of our fallen world. Sometimes hearing a good story can erase a frown, clear confusion, or compel us to act when we are frozen by fear, doubt, or other afflictions.

In the church, we often refer to the gospel of Jesus as "the greatest story ever told." It most certainly is. The effect that stories can have on people is often profound and sometimes even life-changing. This is absolutely the case regarding Christians and our relationship to the gospel or the "good news" of Jesus. In the character of Jesus, we see all of God's character reflected and distilled into one central point, wrapped in human flesh. In Christ, we see a humble servant and God himself at the same time. He is ultimately relatable and yet, simultaneously perfectly holy.

As we follow Christ, the power of the sacrifice of Jesus and how He conquered death echoes throughout our own experiences and reminds us that we can be more than conquerors. We see ourselves in the story of Jesus. We see our sin and redemption intersecting at the cross. In the person of Jesus, we are simultaneously challenged to reach up to a higher standard and yet we find comfort that even though we fail, we can always receive mercy. This from a God who loves us so much that He would give his life for us.

## Identity in the Character of Jesus

Every story has heroes and villains, as well as major and minor characters. Sometimes we're not sure where we fit into the story of creation. Perhaps

---

[1] Please note that the first lesson has been written in a very personal way, direct to the reader. This is by design. We pray it will stir you and encourage you.

we fear we are nothing but background characters—maybe, in the grand scheme of things, we really don't matter. We may think our story isn't too amazing.

"Who am I? I'm nobody."

Yet, this is not how we are regarded by Christ and by the Father: *For God so loved the world, that he gave his only Son, that whoever believes in him should not perish but have eternal life,* John 3.16.

Try substituting "the world" with "me."

> For God so loved *me*, that he gave his only Son, that *I* could believe in him and not perish but have eternal life.

If you are in Christ, there is nothing about your story that is insignificant or unimportant to God. Your story is now part of the family history of God's people. We may identify with our past sins, hang-ups, or struggles. We may also identify with our accomplishments, job titles or role in society. We may even be tempted to compare ourselves to others or wish for a different story than the one we have. God sees a bigger picture than that. To Him, your story matters.

If you are in Christ, the arc of your story has now curved heavenward. It began the moment your sins were washed away.[2] In Christ, there is a new and higher identity. You are God's chosen. You are kept and called to a higher purpose of love, service, and praise. You are a disciple of the good teacher and sheep in the flock of the good shepherd. Your struggles are now and will forever be turned over to the might and power of Jesus Christ. *But you are a chosen race, a royal priesthood, a holy nation, a people for his own possession, that you may proclaim the excellencies of him who called you out of darkness into his marvelous light,* 2 Peter 1.9.

## Tell Your Story

*My mouth will tell of your righteous acts, of your deeds of salvation all the day, for their number is past my knowledge,* Psalm 71.15. Christians who grew up in the church and lived a "normal" church kid's life sometimes feel like their walk with Jesus isn't special or inspirational. Christians who grew up outside of church, or others who departed from Jesus early and left the church behind may feel like they are not good enough for God. They often feel

---

[2] See Acts 22.16.

shame over their past. The truth is this—the background is irrelevant. The most powerful evidence for the supremacy of Christ is a redeemed life. This is something every Christian possesses. Therefore, we ought to praise God for weaving the story that He has in our own lives.

It is not self-centered to share the story of your walk with God, so long as the focus is placed exactly where it belongs. Telling the story of how you came to Christ and what that meant for you may just inspire another to do the very same. If enough people declare the righteousness of God in enough places, then we have a movement. Then we have an Acts of the Apostles sort of culture in our churches. That's why you should tell your story. It might inspire someone. It might encourage them to take that next step of faith.

As such, below are a collection of short stories of the conversions of real people who gave their lives to Christ.[3]

## Mike's Story

Mike grew up going to churches here and there, but never really had a relationship with God until he came across someone at work who stood out to him as an example of Christian conduct. No matter how hard this man was pressured at work to swear or curse, he never would. Mike finally asked him "Why?" His coworker responded with the words of Jesus, Mark 7.15: *"There is nothing outside a person that by going into him can defile him, but the things that come out of a person are what defile him."*

From there, Mike began studying the word with his coworker. Mike got into the Scriptures and started to reorient his life. He thought hard about who he was and where he was going with his life. Eventually he ended up visiting a congregation in suburban Dayton, Ohio, where he met people who welcomed him and showed him kindness. Several months later, Mike and his wife were baptized into Christ after having a Bible study with some of the members there.

Mike went back to work and started to realize he was standing out for the same reason as his friend who originally invited him to church, for better or worse. He admitted he was not perfect, but his outlook on life had changed forever. Knowing there's a long road ahead, he continues to press on every

---

3   These are all retellings, and as such have paraphrases and addendum to the original recorded interviews from which these stories were taken.

day to be more like Jesus. Mike is currently, at the time of writing, a deacon in the Lord's church.

> *"Now I realize I fail, and I can ask forgiveness, wake up the next day and start fresh … Knowing that I sin and what he did for me for those sins … I know he loves me so much, and I could never repay him with the love that I have."*

## Kyle's Story

Kyle grew up in the church but wasn't baptized until he was an adult and in college. His father and grandfather were both Christians and he grew up spending every Sunday in church. It took getting out into the world and seeing how it was to move him to decide to commit to Christ. He had put off baptism until college when, in 2006, he was baptized by his grandfather. Through a rough first couple of years, he struggled with certain "old ways" that had been left behind but ultimately pressed through those struggles.

Now, Christ's sacrifice is a recurring thought for him that keeps pressing him on. Kyle has a background in the military, so the concept of sacrifice resonates strongly with him. Now, internalizing the willingness of Christ to endure that pain and suffering of the cross for all mankind undergirds and continually motivates Kyle's walk. The man-made answers of the world didn't satisfy him. God as a basis is where Kyle has placed his faith. For Kyle, God is a "strong, concrete foundation," for himself and for his family.

> *"Christ is a foundation for life."*

## Amanda's Story

Amanda has been a Christian for more than 27 years. She was raised in a faithful Christian home and eventually baptized at eleven years old. For her, it was a simple mustard-seed sized faith that motivated her to stop her parents in the parking lot to tell them that she wanted to be baptized that night. The next day, she felt like she was "shining from the inside out." Her faith has continually grown and changed since then.

Now, Jesus has colored every aspect of her life. Having that relationship with Jesus and being a part of the family of God has found its way into all her family and work relationships. Jesus has been with her through moves throughout the country, starting a family, struggles with depression and countless other twists and turns. She is a dedicated servant who involves herself in every way possible with the life of the church.

> "Christ was always there ... He was the reason that Chris and I continued to work hard in our marriage. There are a lot of things in my life that probably would have fallen apart without Jesus and the people he sends into our lives ..."

## Jim's Story

Nearing 70 years of faithfulness to Christ, Jim was baptized into Christ in 1952. As he was being apprenticed to become an electrician, he was assigned to a mentor who influenced him for Christ. Jim had some church background but for the most part, hadn't had any sort of relationship with God. One day he was approached by some relatives about baptizing his children. When Jim shared this conversation with the man who was mentoring him at work, he responded, "What do those children believe?"

That spurred a series of new questions and conversations. Every free minute on the job, that fellow shared Jesus' teachings with Jim. He shared with him about believer's baptism. Jim and his wife, Vera, eventually had the man in their home for a Bible study where they all dove into the Bible together over a course of many weeks. He continually kept inviting them to church.

Eventually, Jim and Vera attended a church of Christ in the town where they were. They had questions about the singing, communion, and several other practices. A few things stood out to them. It wasn't long before they were being invited to social gatherings with the members of the church there. Jim described being impressed with their conduct and their attitude of kindness and holiness.

After hearing enough preaching and teaching, and spending time with those Christians, it came to the moment that Jim and Vera were ready to turn their lives over to Jesus. The invitation was given one Sunday morning, and after Bible study and prayer, they went forward and were baptized into Christ. He and Vera enjoyed many years of a loving marriage and service to God together before she went home to be with the Lord. To this day, their children, grandchildren, and even great grandchildren continue to carry the banner of the cross. Out of this legacy have come elders, preachers, teachers, and dedicated servants of the Lord.

> "I not only have a good physical family, but a large percentage of them are also a part of my spiritual family ... and that gives me comfort. I intend and pray that when I leave this world, that I will be in line to receive that same gift that I'm confident Vera's given."

## For Thought and Reflection

1. Why are stories so powerful?

2. What makes a good story?

3. What is the gospel?

4. How does the gospel fit into the story of your life?

5. How can sharing your story with others help them get to know Jesus? Why should we tell our own story?

# Lesson 2

# The Magnitude of Your Salvation

## Coming to Appreciate What You Have Been Given in Christ

## Introduction

Hear. Believe. Repent. Confess. Be Baptized. These steps of salvation have been something you may have heard from your earliest of years.

What are the five acts of worship? If you answer singing, preaching, prayer, giving, and partaking of the Lord's Supper, you'd be correct.

What is the work of the church? Evangelism, edification, and benevolence summarizes it point by point.

It is probably safe to say that those in and around the churches of Christ over the last century are familiar with these lists. And perhaps, maybe you've heard these systems of salvation, worship, and work taught in comparison with denominational practices, sometimes with the impression being left that those with differing viewpoints have bad hearts and are willfully being dishonest with Scripture. Our system is so easy to see, *why can't others see it*?

Summarizing biblical doctrine in such succinct manners is not always bad. They are good points to emphasize. However, there is the need that we see these matters not just from the perspective of being part of a system that differentiates us from other believers in the religious world, but rather as a heartfelt response to an amazing God who has gone out of His way to save us from eternity's fire. A heavy concentration on a *system* or *procedure* can have drawbacks. Religion is not only a matter of logic. Bringing others to salvation is not just about winning convincing arguments and using powerful words. Evangelistic outreach involves the head *and* the heart.

The heart. An emotional connection to Jesus. Think of how many people who are, year in and year out, led to the baptistry. We rejoice with them as they exit the water… then we never see them again. What happened? Could it be that we did a good job making a logical connection in convincing them to respond to a system, but somewhere along the line we failed in making a connection to their heart? Having an emotional connection to Jesus and the salvation He provides is something we must all help facilitate with every lost person who is considering repentance and baptism.

It doesn't matter if you've just become a Christian, or if you have been one for many years, it is of vital importance to grasp the significance of your salvation. At the time of your baptism, you may not have fully understood the entire magnitude of your decision, but your heart should have been touched by God's extreme love and work in reestablishing the relationship you lost after sin invaded your life.

## The Magnitude of Stepping Into the Light

Over the course of my life, I've had the opportunity to visit several caves administered and protected by the National Park Service as well as some in various state parks around the country. A few that I've visited are Blanchard Springs in Arkansas, Mammoth Cave in Kentucky, Ohio Caverns in …Ohio, and Jewell Cave in South Dakota. They're all reasonably safe, well lit, and full of stairs. As you traverse the cave, you are always under the watchful eye of a park ranger. They make sure to point out all the points of interest along the way. The beauty is amazing. They are all special in their own unique way. On every tour I've ever been, the ranger is sure to stop the group at the deepest point and turn off the lights. If you've never been inside a cave with no lighting, it is hard to imagine the gravity of the darkness. The feeling you have can be overwhelming. There is always relief when the lights come back on.

The one wild cave I've been in is on the western slope of the Black Hills, known as Bear Trap Cave. It's a completely different experience from the well-manicured and supervised National Park Caves. Rather than an expansive door to walk through or elevator to go down, this journey begins by dropping down into a hole out in the middle of a burned-out forest, 50 miles from the nearest town. Once inside, a person must crouch as they walk back about 20 feet before going down a steep incline to a very large room that has at least a 40-foot ceiling. There is no lighting. The path is full of rocks and jagged boulders. As you descend into the large room, there is a cliff off to the left with jagged rocks and boulders on the floor below. The gravel is like walking on marbles. Its treacherous. You would never want to go into this place by yourself. And, unlike the National Park Caves, this is just a hole in the ground … there is not much beauty inside.

A few years ago, a friend of mine ventured into Bear Trap Cave for the first time ... alone. After he got in so far, his flashlight went out, and before he knew it, he had stumbled over the cliff falling to the floor 40 feet below. He was knocked out. After coming to, lying on the floor of this giant room in great pain and having difficulty breathing, my friend spent the first few minutes preparing to die. He had several broken ribs and ankle. There was no light. He had no clue on how to get out. No one knew where he was. It was winter and could have been weeks before anyone would have come upon his truck parked topside. He figured he had reached the end of the line. He thought of his family and the trauma they would soon be going through. He was angry at himself for getting in this situation. He prayed. He prayed some more.

After what seemed like hours, he crawled, in total darkness, a few feet over to touch and feel his way out ... hopefully finding a way leading up. When he got around a large crevice, to his great relief, was a ray of light emanating from the cave entrance a hundred feet away. As he continued to crawl around, he finally found the way back up and followed the light. Brighter and brighter, it became. Finally, he was able to get himself out of the cave and drive himself to the hospital. Prayers answered.

After such an experience can you imagine what it would be like to come up to the top and get back into the daylight? That magnitude of the moment would be something you'd never forget. You'd never forget the feeling. A hopeless situation was now one of deliverance. Now there is the opportunity to embrace a second chance at life. Emotional? Absolutely.

Now, let's make the application to the spiritual.

## The Romans' Emotional Response to the Gospel

In Romans 6.17 Paul commends the Roman Christians for the way they came to Christ. He says: *But thank God that, although you used to be slaves of sin, you obeyed from the heart that pattern of teaching to which you were handed over.*

Note how the Romans were motivated out of the heart to obediently respond to the gospel. From the heart describes a very personal decision one makes, by his own volition, to surrender to God. But Paul's words go farther. He is not speaking of superficial or coerced obedience, but rather something deeply felt and deeply motivated from deep inside someone.[4] The Christian reality is a matter of the heart. Paul focused on this in at least two other places in Romans:

- Romans 5.5: This hope will not disappoint us, because God's love has been poured out in our hearts through the Holy Spirit who was given to us.
- Romans 10.9-10: If you confess with your mouth, "Jesus is Lord," and believe in your heart that God raised him from the dead, you will be saved. One believes with the heart, resulting in righteousness, and one confesses with the mouth, resulting in salvation.

Paul's emphasis on the heart makes sense when we think about salvation by grace through faith. We have been released from the penalty of law and thereby deemed "not guilty." How can we not be impacted to our very core when we read *there is now no condemnation for those in Christ Jesus,* Romans 8.1? Salvation by grace is a matter of the heart.

# What You Received the Day You Became a Christian

## Light

*For you were once darkness, but now you are light in the Lord. Walk as children of light,* Ephesians 5.8. Just like my friend who walked out of what could have been a dark cave of death, spiritually, you were brought out of darkness and into the eternal light of Jesus Christ.

- Isaiah 9.2, 4: The people walking in darkness have seen a great light; a light has dawned on those living in the land of darkness. …For you have shattered their oppressive yoke and the rod on their shoulders, the staff of their oppressor, just as you did on the day of Midian.
- John 12.46: I have come as light into the world, so that everyone who believes in me would not remain in darkness.

## A Relationship

Through the blood of Jesus, our **hostility** has been replaced with **peace**, Ephesians 2.14. We are no longer **aliens**, but **citizens**, 2.19. We are no longer **strangers**, but members of **God's household**, 2.19. This was all made

---

4  Dunn, James D. G. *Romans 1–8.* Vol. 38A. Word Biblical Commentary. Dallas: Word, Incorporated, 1988, p. 343.

possible through the riches of God's **mercy**. Because of His great **love**, while we were **dead** in our trespasses and sins, God made us **alive** together with Christ. By **grace** we have been saved, and we have been **raised** up with Him and **seated** with Him in the heavenly places, Ephesians 2.4-6a.

The day of your salvation was the most momentous day of your life. On that day you received:

- **The Father,** who knows your name. While this passage has an immediate application to the redemption of Israel, its ultimate application is for all who desire to be a part of spiritual Israel: *Now this is what the Lord says— the one who created you, Jacob, and the one who formed you, Israel— "Do not fear, for I have redeemed you;* **I have called you by your name; you are mine***,* Isaiah 43.1.
- **Jesus**: *Now if* **Christ is in you**, *the body is dead because of sin, but the Spirit gives life because of righteousness,* Romans 8.10.
- **The Spirit**: *Don't you know that your body is a temple of* **the Holy Spirit who is in you**, *whom you have from God? You are not your own,* 1 Corinthians 6.19.

## The Word of God

This is the instrument the Spirit continues to use on us long after our salvation: *This is why we constantly thank God, because when you received the word of God that you heard from us, you welcomed it not as a human message, but as it truly is, the word of God, which also works effectively in you who believe,* 1 Thessalonians 2.13. What a blessing that as we allow the word to *dwell within us richly,* Colossians 3.16a, we have a guidebook to get us through the rigors of life.

## Talents and Gifts

You have been given non-miraculous gifts and abilities to use in service to others and for the glorification of God. *Just as each one has received a gift, use it to serve others, as good stewards of the varied grace of God,* 1 Peter 4.10.

## Newness & Forgiveness

What you did before, doesn't matter anymore. It's all been forgiven. You have been remade. You are now the workmanship of God. *Therefore, if anyone is in*

*Christ, he is a new creation; the old has passed away, and see, the new has come,* 2 Corinthians 5.17.

In 1 Corinthians 6.9-11 Paul expresses it this way:

> Don't you know that the unrighteous will not inherit God's kingdom? Do not be deceived: No sexually immoral people, idolaters, adulterers, or males who have sex with males, no thieves, greedy people, drunkards, verbally abusive people, or swindlers will inherit God's kingdom. And some of you used to be like this. But you were washed, you were sanctified, you were justified in the name of the Lord Jesus Christ and by the Spirit of our God.

In Ephesians 1.7 Paul summarizes it thusly: *In him we have redemption through his blood, the forgiveness of our trespasses, according to the riches of his grace.*

## Conclusion

All these things are worthy of an emotional response. The God of the universe loved us enough to do everything possible for us to spend eternity with Him. *It is so much more than obedience to a system of doctrine; it is about you and God together for all of eternity!* It is about our heart being given over to God.

Do you realize the magnitude of your salvation?

## For Thought and Reflection

1. What are some of the drawbacks of emphasizing a system over touching a heart?

2. What does *from the heart* describe in Romans 6.17?

3. Why do you think Paul emphasizes the heart so much in Romans?

4. What kind of emotional reaction should Romans 8.1 generate within us?

5. How has being brought into the light been a blessing for you?

6. Describe the impact of having a relationship with our Lord. As you approach each day, what does this mean to you?

7. How special is it that the Father knows your name?

8. How has receiving the Word of God changed your life?

9. How has using the gifts/talents given to you by the Spirit enriched your Christian experience in the service of others?

10. How has your knowledge of being made new and being forgiven changed your perspective on life?

## Lesson 3
# Defining New Testament Christianity
### Following the Example of the First Christians

## Introduction

*Hold on to the pattern of sound teaching that you have heard from me, in the faith and love that are in Christ Jesus. Guard the good deposit through the Holy Spirit who lives in us,* 2 Timothy 1.13–14.

2 Timothy is largely thought to be Paul's final letter. Written from a prison cell in Rome, this very personal letter to Timothy instructs the young evangelist to hold on to (preserve or keep) the teaching he had received from Paul. In verse 14, it is called *the good deposit*. Timothy was told to treat it in such a way that it would not be lost or damaged. It was of vital importance because he had been given the true gospel, which Paul had directly received from Christ Himself, Galatians 1.1, 12; 2.7. And now, the directive is for Timothy to teach it to others. *What you have heard from me in the presence of many witnesses, commit to faithful men who will be able to teach others also,* 2 Timothy 2.2.

Why is "sound teaching" of such importance?

## Devoted to the Apostles' Teaching

Going back to the beginning of the church in Acts 2, Luke tells us the early church devoted itself *to the apostles' teaching,* Acts 2.42. The *apostles' teaching* was the standard. As the gospel spread into Gentile areas, Paul told the Corinthians he had sent Timothy to them for the purpose of being a reminder of *my ways in Christ Jesus, just as I teach everywhere in every church,* 1 Corinthians 4.17. Thus, we see the basis for doctrinal unity: the same thing was taught among all the churches. Anything other than the apostles' teaching was to be rejected. *We are from God. Anyone who knows God listens to us; anyone who is not from God does not listen to us. This is how we know the Spirit of truth and the spirit of deception,* 1 John 4.6.

There is truth. There is deception. One way is right. Any other way is wrong. Erroneous ways and teachings are to be strictly avoided, Galatians 1.6–9; 2 Thessalonians 3.6. Paul instructed the Romans: *watch out for those who create divisions and obstacles contrary to the teaching that you learned. Avoid them,* Romans 16.17.

The apostles' teaching serves as the God-given standard by which everything else must be measured. We are to:

- *Hold fast to it,* 2 Timothy 1.13; 1 Corinthians 11.2; 2 Thessalonians 2.15.
- *Guard it,* 2 Timothy 1.14.
- *Contend for it,* Jude 3.

## The Apostles' Teaching Is to Be Followed

When Paul says in 1.13 to *hold on to the pattern of sound teaching that you have heard from me,* he is intending for Timothy to view the teaching of the apostles as a prototype, sketch, outline, example, or standard.[5] *Pattern* means "a blow," and was used of the impression left by a horse's hoof, a seal, or an engraved mark. It conveyed the image of a model by which one could "maintain the sameness of a thing."[6]

The "sound teaching" of 2 Timothy 1.13 can be broadly described as the teaching of Jesus Christ revealed by Himself or via inspiration of the Spirit by the Apostles. Once we have followed the Great Commission and made disciples, Matthew 28.19, there is more to do. *Teaching,* Matthew 28.20, is the second half of the great commission. Newly converted saints are to be instructed *to observe everything* Jesus commanded.

Jesus referred to His teaching as life: *The words that I have spoken to you are spirit and are life,* John 6.63b. Just before Paul told Timothy to hold on to sound teaching, he said Jesus *brought life and immortality to light through the gospel,* 2 Timothy 1.10. So, the conclusion is obvious: to have *life* and *immortality* ... we must follow the teachings set forth in the New Testament. However, it is not just about the teaching or dissemination of information;

---

5   Arndt, William, Frederick W. Danker, Walter Bauer, and F. Wilbur Gingrich. *A Greek-English Lexicon of the New Testament and Other Early Christian Literature.* Chicago: University of Chicago Press, 2000, p. 1042. Here afterward, this reference will be abbreviated using the term BDAG.

6   Wuest, Kenneth S. *Wuest's Word Studies from the Greek New Testament: For the English Reader.* Grand Rapids: Eerdmans, 1997, Vol. 8, p. 125.

God's word must be adhered to as a heartfelt response. Note how Paul commended Timothy when he said, *you have **followed** my teaching, conduct, purpose, faith, patience, love, and endurance,* 2 Timothy 3.10.

How did the early church follow the apostles' teaching?

## In Moral Conduct

Jesus is the ultimate example who not only revealed truth but also lived it perfectly, Hebrews 4.15. The apostles also held themselves up as examples to follow. Going back to 2 Timothy 1.13, Paul's life and teachings were to be a model for Christian living in everyday life. He wrote: *Join in imitating me, brothers and sisters, and pay careful attention to those who live according to the example you have in us,* Philippians 3.17. The believers in Thessalonica were also said to have provided an example for believers in other places: *As a result, you became an example to all the believers in Macedonia and Achaia,* 1 Thessalonians 1.7.

The Christian lifestyle is remarkably different from the world. We are salt and light, Matthew 5.13–14, and are called to *walk just as He walked,* 1 John 2.6. This is the general principle behind Paul's instruction to Timothy and Titus:

- 2 Timothy 4.12b: Set an example for the believers in speech, in conduct, in love, in faith, and in purity.
- Titus 2.7: Make yourself an example of good works with integrity and dignity in your teaching.

## In Doctrine

Romans 6.17–18 is notable. Paul expressed his great thanks that the Roman Christians had *obeyed from the heart that pattern of teaching to which you were handed over.* In the previous lesson, we learned how the gospel message impacted those in Rome to the core of their being. Their hearts were touched which caused them to naturally respond to the teachings of the gospel. When a person becomes a Christian he or she is *handed over* or "placed under the authority of" Christian teaching … the expression of God's will for believers. It is not that the teaching has been handed over to us … we have been handed over to it.[7] *The teaching* serves as the standard to

---

7   Moo, Douglas J. *The Epistle to the Romans.* The New International Commentary on the New Testament. Grand Rapids, MI: Wm. B. Eerdmans Publishing Co., 1996, p.401.

follow. Biblical doctrine molds and forms those who have been handed over to it.[8]

In this way, apostolic teachings can be likened to a mold, like a form for concrete.[9] When concrete is poured, it sets up around the form created for it. The form holds it in place and makes it distinctive. When we do what the apostles did to form churches in the first century, we will plant the same type of churches today. Thinking doctrinally, when we follow the New Testament, we will teach the same form of teaching the apostles used. Following the apostles' teaching facilitates our spiritual stability and growth. *Then we will no longer be little children, tossed by the waves and blown around by every wind of teaching, by human cunning with cleverness in the techniques of deceit,* Ephesians 4.14. Christians are rooted in the apostles' teachings, which is stable, secure, and unchanging.

### What Are Some of the Specific Doctrines Taught By the Apostles?

- The inspiration and authority of Scripture, 1 Thessalonians 2.13.
- The deity and humanity of Christ, Philippians 2.6–7; Colossians 1.15–16.
- Atonement, Romans 3.25–28; 1 Peter 1.18–21.
- Justification by grace through faith, Romans 4–5.
- Baptism for the remission of sin, Acts 2.38; Colossians 2.11–14; 1 Peter 3.21.
- The organization of the church, i.e., elders, deacons, and saints, Philippians 1.1.
- The Christian lifestyle, Philippians 2.15–16a.
- Worship, *in spirit and truth,* John 4.24.
- The Lord's Supper, Matthew 26.26–30.
- Jesus' return, 2 Peter 3.8–10; 1 Thessalonians 4.11–16.
- The resurrection, 1 Corinthians 15.
- The judgment to come, Hebrews 9.27.

---

8   Kittel, Gerhard, Geoffrey W. Bromiley, and Gerhard Friedrich, eds. *Theological Dictionary of the New Testament.* Grand Rapids, MI: Eerdmans, 1964–, Vol. 8, p. 250.

9   Wharton, Edward. *The Church of Christ: The Distinctive Nature of the New Testament Church.* Nashville: Gospel Advocate Company, 1997, p. 14–15. Wharton uses the analogy of a mold, cast, or form for Christians to follow so that they can "identify the saved from the lost, and consequently give the church its distinct identity as the saved body of Christ."

- Eternal life or eternal condemnation, Matthew 25.46.[10]

## "One Faith"

In Ephesians 4.3 Paul makes a call for unity. The desire for *peace*, driven by our love for Christ and one another keeps us together. Beginning with verse 4, Paul lists several areas where Christians are to hold common conviction: *There is one body and one Spirit—just as you were called to one hope at your calling—one Lord, one faith, one baptism, one God and Father of all, who is above all and through all and in all*, Ephesians 4.4–6.

A few verses later Paul says that we can come to a knowledge and unity of *the faith*, 4.13. In this case, we are referring to faith in a noun sense, i.e., a system or thing to be identified and contrasted to other things. The term is singular. A search of the New Testament where *the faith* is used reveals that it is to be:

- *Preached*, Galatians 1.23.
- *Obeyed*, Acts 6.7.
- *Continued* in, Acts 14.22.
- *Strengthened in*, Acts 16.5.
- *Contended for* together, Philippians 1.27.
- *Be grounded and steadfast in,* Colossians 1.23.
- *Established in,* Colossians 2.7.
- *Nourished by the words of,* 1 Timothy 4.6.
- *Fought for,* 1 Timothy 6.12.
- *Contended for,* Jude 3.

It can be *departed from*, 1 Timothy 4.1; *denied*, 1 Timothy 5.8; and a person can go *astray* from it, 1 Timothy 6.21.

The New Testament knows of only one faith. *The faith* is something objective and absolute. We are expected to unite around it. Where we do not agree, we must apply the principles of Ephesians 4.2–3, i.e., we practice *patience* and *humility,* and *we bear with one another in love* for the purpose of maintaining the unity God has given. A divisive spirit is foreign to New Testament Christianity.

---

10  Wharton, p. 19. I have added a few scripture references to his excellent list of NT doctrine.

## How We Follow

Paul's teaching in Colossians also emphasizes the need to become established firmly. But also, he does not neglect to mention the motivation of the heart: *So then, just as you have received Christ Jesus as Lord, continue to walk in him, being rooted and built up in him and established in the faith, just as you were taught, and* **overflowing with gratitude**, Colossians 2.6–7. The thought of what has been done on our behalf should never be too far from our minds.

This naturally follows to our possession of a spirit of gentleness, humility, and love. In 2 Timothy 1.13b, Paul told Timothy to hand off what he received in the same way he had received it: *in the faith and love that are in Christ Jesus.*

*How* one holds on to the sound words is also of vital importance.

## With Humility

When we communicate these concepts, speaking with clarity, certainty, and exclusivity, we must check our attitude. We must never give off an impression that the churches of Christ are perfect, have arrived, and have no more work to do in study and practice. Our work and understanding of Biblical teaching is never finished. We must always teach and exhort with the strongest sense of humility: *For by the grace given to me, I tell everyone among you not to think of himself more highly than he should think. Instead, think sensibly, as God has distributed a measure of faith to each one,* Romans 12.3.

We can, in the spirit of humility and love, make the distinction between what has been divinely revealed as truth and that which is of human origin. We have not been called to compromise or negotiate with beliefs that set themselves up against what has been revealed. Instead, we are to, as Paul taught in Romans 6.17, *submit ourselves to the form of teaching to which we have been handed over.* God's revealed truth is that by which we are molded. We should unashamedly call upon our religious friends to unite with us in the pursuit of God's truth as revealed by Christ and His apostles.

## In Faith

We are to hold on to it *in faith,* i.e., earnestly believing that what we have received is in accordance with God's will and revealed word. *The faith,* or the teachings we have received have power. It has changed our life, and we want it to change others.

## With Love, Optimism, and Joy

As *the faith* was given to us *in love,* so we transmit it in the same way to others. As we teach, we must never be dismissive of or disregard someone's heart, implying that they are a bad person. Instead, we teach *in love,* optimism, and joy, highlighting how these teachings have the power to truly transform a person into the image of Christ.

# For Thought and Reflection

1. What was so important about the teaching Timothy had received from Paul?

2. What is *sound teaching?*

3. Why must *sound teaching* be followed?

4. What kind of example was Timothy to set in moral conduct? What is the expectation for us?

5. What does it mean that we have been *handed over* to a pattern of teaching? (Romans 6.17)

6. What does the sound doctrine of 2 Timothy 1.13 encompass? Can you think of additional things?

7. What is the basis of doctrinal unity?

8. Is it possible to come to a unity of the faith? (See Ephesians 4.13) Explain.

9. How are we to proceed regarding the things on which we do not agree?

10. Is the work of restoration ever finished?

11. What is the model we look to when thinking of restoring the New Testament church?

12. What does it mean to move *in faith* and *in love* when sharing the *sound words* of the gospel?

Lesson 4

# Identifying the New Testament Church

## Introduction

*And I also say to you that you are Peter, and on this rock I will build my church, and the gates of Hades will not overpower it*, Matthew 16.18.

As Matthew 16 begins, Jesus is being subjected to another test by the Pharisees and Sadducees who demanded a sign from heaven. After rebuking them, He and the disciples head to the other shore of the sea of Galilee and from there to Caesarea Philippi. This region would have offered a welcome break from the large crowds and constant attention of Jesus' enemies. This provided Jesus the opportunity to be alone with the disciples and find much-needed personal time for instruction and encouragement.

The area where they traveled was mostly non-Jewish. Caesarea Philippi was around 25 miles northeast of the Sea of Galilee. The area contained many temples dedicated to ancient Syrian Baal-worship. William Barclay mentions one source that says there were as many as 14 of these temples in the area.[11] Besides that, this was also the home of the Syrian gods. Just outside the gates of the city was a great hill, and deep inside it was a cavern that was said to be the birthplace of the great god Pan, the god of nature. All of this was woven into the area's identity as Caesarea Philippi's original name was Panias.

Here also was the source of the river Jordan, which would have had great significance to any Jew who cared about their religious heritage. *The ancient faith of Judaism would be in the air for anyone who was a devout and pious Jew.*[12] There are a great number of stories and events of Old Testament Judaism tied to the Jordan River. But finally, in this area, Herod the Great constructed a great temple and dedicated it to the godhood of Caesar. The building was made of white marble and built on a mountain where it could be seen for miles around from any direction. This temple was a proud monument to the might of Rome with all its gods and Caesars proclaiming its power.

---

11 Barclay, William. *The Gospel of Matthew*. Third Ed. The New Daily Study Bible. Edinburgh: Saint Andrew Press, 2001, p. 156.

12 Barclay, p. 156.

Now, let's return to Jesus and the twelve. They are standing in the outskirts of the city, Mark 8.27. Jesus has just spent time alone in prayer, Luke 9.18. Time is of the essence because the cross is rapidly approaching. He has so much to teach and train them before He goes. Could they elevate their perspective and think spiritually? It would be difficult, as it is for all humans. Their present circumstances weren't too desirable. By earthly standards they had nothing. No money. No education. No social status. The religious establishment was seeking to destroy them. Those with political power looked at them wearily and cast a suspicious eye. And it is here, in the same area where the world's religions were all represented, He asked them if they believed He was the Son of God. Barclay writes:

> It is as if Jesus deliberately set himself against the background of the world's religions in all their history and their splendour and demanded to be compared with them and to have the verdict given in his favour. There are few scenes where Jesus' consciousness of his own divinity shines out with a more dazzling light.[13]

We know the text. After a brief discussion of who people thought the Messiah was, Jesus asks, *who do you say that I am?* Without hesitation, Peter answered: *You are the Messiah, the Son of the living God,* Matthew 16.16. Jesus goes on to say that this had been revealed to Peter by the Father and then He says *that upon this rock,* i.e., this confession of truth, *Jesus is the Son of God,* He would build His church. There is so much wrapped into this confession. When we come to Christ and confess that He is the Son of God, we are making a profound statement of our belief and trust in:

- Him being our Savior from sin, Luke 19.10.
- Him being *the way, the truth,* and *the life,* and the only way to access the Father, John 14.6.

After the cross, the church would be built on the foundation of the apostles and prophets with Jesus being the chief cornerstone: *So, then, you are no longer foreigners and strangers, but fellow citizens with the saints, and members of God's household, built on the foundation of the apostles and prophets, with Christ Jesus himself as the cornerstone,* Ephesians 2.20.

Peter, in 1 Peter 2.6, uses the imagery from Isaiah 28.16 to describe the building of the church. *The one who believes will be unshakable.* Paul says this structure serves as a habitation of God in the Spirit, Ephesians 2.21–22.

---

13   Barclay, p. 158.

Going back to Matthew 16.18, this is where we first observe the word "church" used in the New Testament.[14] Jesus' statement in this context is not so much about *when* the church would be established (the disciples would have had no concept about Pentecost yet) but with *the certainty* that the church would be established. No matter what happened, not even His death, would stop the coming of the church. God would build it. The Father would have His *called-out ones*. God would have *His people*. The disciples needed to see they were part of something that would never fail. And so are we today. Countries may rise and fall, but God's church will go on until He calls it home.

## Defining "Church"

There are over 100 different terms, metaphors, and images used inside the New Testament to describe God's *people*, i.e., those with whom He has entered a saving relationship. In preparing this study, I browsed through a few church bulletins and periodicals circulated within the churches of Christ over the last 70 years. The vast majority contain the truth but are written in a way that is only concerned with differentiating the Lord's church from denominationalism. Many miss, in my opinion, the very special relationship, purpose, and place that God has called the church to. We are not part of some cold, strictly organized, and mechanical organization ... we are part of the living and dynamic family of God, who has called us out of darkness to be His special people ... His sons and daughters. We are the "called out body of people who belong to the Lord. He has called (us) out of one realm and into another."[15] We need to make it personal and feel the warmth of God's love and desire for having *a people* that is His very own.

### As a Secular Reference

"Church" as used in Matthew 16.18, has a long history in the Greek-speaking world. *Ekklēsia* comes from a compound word that means "out of a calling." In the earliest Greek writings, it is seen as a verb used to summon an army to assemble. From the 5th century B.C. on, it was commonly used as a political term to refer to the assembly "of full citizens, ... in which political and

---

14  "Church" is used only twice in the gospels, here in Matthew 16.18 and also in Matthew 18.17.

15  Wharton, p. 39.

judicial decisions were taken."[16] One New Testament example where we see the word used secularly is found in Acts 19.32 where an illegal "assembly" gathered in support of the silversmiths of Artemis who wanted Paul, Gaius, and Aristarchus killed. *Ekklēsia* is used here to describe the mob that had been called out of the marketplace and into the amphitheater to riot.

First century historians Josephus and Philo use *ekklēsia* quite often in their writings. They use it to describe *gatherings of people* comprised of religious, political, or other types of assemblies. **The connotation did not refer to an organization or society.**

## As a Spiritual Reference

It is Paul who first takes the secular term so common in his day and uses it in a spiritual sense to refer to God's people. He uses it to describe:

### A Local Group of Believers

Thinking chronologically, Paul's first usage of *ekklēsia* appears in 1 Thessalonians 1.1 as he greets the saints in Thessalonica:[17] *Paul, Silvanus, and Timothy: To the church of the Thessalonians in God the Father and the Lord Jesus Christ. Grace to you and peace.*

Note here how Paul describes the unique identity of *assembly* or *gathering* in Thessalonica. They are *in God the Father and the Lord Jesus Christ*. They belong to God. Not only that, but they are also in Christ. Those in the *ekklēsia* wear His name. They have been called from the kingdom of darkness and transferred to the kingdom of Christ, Colossians 1.13.

Their assembling was not just something in theoretical terms … it was something that could be physically identified. *Ekklēsia* applies to "an actual gathering of people, or to a group that gathers when viewed as a

---

16   O'Brien, Peter T. "Church." Edited by Gerald F. Hawthorne, Ralph P. Martin, and Daniel G. Reid. *Dictionary of Paul and His Letters*. Downers Grove, IL: InterVarsity Press, 1993, p. 123.

17   Scholars assert that 1 Thessalonians is the "oldest document in the New Testament," therefore it is the first of Paul's writings to the churches, dating to around 49–51 C.E.

See Ascough, Richard S. *1 & 2 Thessalonians: An Introduction and Study Guide (Encountering the Christ Group at Thessalonike)*. Edited by Tat-siong Benny Liew. Vol. 13. T&T Clark Study Guides to the New Testament. London; Oxford; New York; New Delhi; Sydney: Bloomsbury T&T Clark: An Imprint of Bloomsbury Publishing Plc; Bloomsbury, 2017, p. 3.

regularly constituted meeting."[18] When these people gathered for worship and fellowship, Paul expected his writing to be read *to all the brothers and sisters,* 1 Thessalonians 5.27, and to greet one another *with a holy kiss,* 5.26. Throughout the New Testament we find the apostles specifying local churches in places all over Europe and Asia. For example, we read of churches in Galatia, Judea, Corinth, Thessalonica, etc.

### A Wider Body of Believers

Paul liked to use the body as a metaphor to describe our relationship to Christ.[19] It is prevalent throughout his writing. *The body* can refer to a local congregation in one place,[20] the relationship of Christians with one another,[21] separate local congregations within a geographical area,[22] and finally, a worldwide membership or universal way that includes all Christians.[23] Thinking of this last sense, we are describing "the totality of God's people under the New Covenant."[24]

There are a few places where we could apply *ekklēsia* in the universal sense. Here are a few specific examples:

- Matthew 16.18: *upon this rock I will build my church.*
- Romans 12.4–5: *Now as we have many parts in one body, and all the parts do not have the same function, in the same way we who are many are one body in Christ and individually members of one another.*
- Ephesians 1.22–23: God has *appointed him as head over everything for the church …*
- Ephesians 5.23: *Christ is the head of the church …*
- 1 Timothy 3.15: Paul wrote to Timothy so that he would know how *people ought to conduct themselves in God's household, which is the church of the living God …*

---

18   Ascough, p. 124.

19   See Ephesians 1.22–23; Colossians 1.18; 1 Corinthians 12.13.

20   1 Corinthians 12.27.

21   Inside and outside the local congregation. Romans 12.4–5 can refer to Christian relationships within the same congregation, as well as a wider fellowship outside of the local congregation.

22   Revelation 2–3: The seven churches of Asia.

23   1 Corinthians 12.13.

24   Lewis, Jack P. *Basic Beliefs:* Nashville: 21$^{st}$ Century Christian, 2013, p. 199.

## Other Terms Used to Describe Those in the Church

1 Thessalonians 1.1, 2.1: those who are **in Christ**. If a person is in Christ, he or she is in the church.

Acts 2.47: **those who are saved**. *Every day the Lord added to their number those who were being saved.* Those who respond in faith, repentance, and baptism are added to the number of those who are being saved.

Romans 8.16–17; 1 Timothy 3.15: If we think of God as the Father of us all, and ourselves as brethren and joint heirs with Christ Jesus, then we constitute the **family** or *household* **of God,** *which is the church of the living God, the pillar and foundation of the truth.*[25]

2 Corinthians 5.18–19: Those who have been **reconciled,** *into one body,* Ephesians 2.16. The enmity between God and those in the church has been removed by Jesus' payment for sin on the cross.

1 Peter 1.18–19: Those who have been **purchased** by Christ's blood. See also Ephesians 1.7. If we wish to identify the church of the New Testament, we can do so by finding all who have been bought back from the slavery of sin by the payment Jesus made on the cross.

1 Corinthians 1.1–2: Those who are being **sanctified in Christ Jesus.** To be sanctified means to be set apart from sin. Here Paul calls every Christian a "saint." New Testament Christians behave differently from the world, 1 Peter 1.15. See also Philippians 1.1.

Acts 11.26: the first Christians were known as **disciples.** They were followers and imitators of Jesus Christ.

Acts 9.2: Christians were also called **the Way.** They did so because they followed Jesus, who described Himself as *the way* to life, John 14.6.[26]

## The Singular Nature of the Church

Scripture only knows of one church. *Now as we have many parts in one body, and all the parts do not have the same function, in the same way we who are*

---

[25] Wilson, L. R. "The New Testament Church: Its Terms of Designation." *Gospel Spotlight*, Vol. XVI, Number 28, 7/15/2001, p. 2.

[26] Wharton has a much more detailed list, p. 42–43.

*many are one body in Christ and individually members of one another,* Romans 12.4–5.

These verses have a dual application, one being for life inside the local church, and the other as a wider focus to Christians everywhere. This is the same thought expressed in 1 Corinthians 12.13. Although we may be identified with a specific local congregation, every Christian has been *baptized into one body* by one Spirit.

Note the following passages which identify only one church:

- Ephesians 5.23: *Christ is the savior of **the** body.*
- Colossians 1.18: *He is the head of **the** body.*
- Ephesians 1.23: The church is ***His body**, the fullness of him who fills all in all.*
- Ephesians 4.4–6: *There is **one body** and one Spirit—just as you were called to one hope at your calling—one Lord, one faith, one baptism, one God and Father of all, who is above all and through all and in all.*

## For Thought and Reflection

1. Describe some of the historical background surrounding Matthew 16.14–18.

2. Who is the chief cornerstone of the church?

3. Where is the first usage of "church" in the New Testament? What is the main point of Jesus' teaching?

4. Why is it essential to describe the church in terms of "being the body of those who belong to the Lord?"

5. On what occasion in the New Testament is *ekklēsia* used in a secular sense?

6. When used to refer to a local body of believers, to what does *ekklēsia* refer?

7. Can *ekklēsia* be used to describe a wider body of churches? Explain.

8. How are Christians described in Romans 8.16 & 1 Timothy 3.15? What is the significance of this?

9. How are Christians described in 1 Corinthians 1.1–2 & Philippians 1.1? What is the significance of this?

10. How many churches are identified in Scripture? Why is the important to know?

11. What is an effective way, in your opinion, to teach these things to a modern audience without turning them off?

# Lesson 5
# How to Be Added to the Church

## Introduction

When it comes to salvation, the world can be divided into two distinct categories. A person is either *in Christ* (saved and identified as a Christian) or out of Christ (lost and not a Christian). Out of Christ, one is *without hope and without God in the world*, Ephesians 2.12.

Paul loved to speak of being *in Christ*. Throughout his writing, he uses the term to stress where salvation is and identify the many blessings that come as a result. Here are a few examples:

- 2 Corinthians 5.17: *Therefore, if anyone is **in Christ**, he is a **new creation**; the old has passed away, and see, the new has come.*
- Romans 8.1: *Therefore, there is now no condemnation for those **in Christ Jesus**.*
- Romans 6.23: *For the wages of sin is death, but the gift of God is **eternal life in Christ Jesus** our Lord.*
- 2 Timothy 2.10: *This is why I endure all things for the elect: so that they also may obtain **salvation**, which is **in Christ Jesus**, with eternal glory.*
- Ephesians 1.7: ***In him** we have **redemption** through his blood, the **forgiveness** of our trespasses, according to the riches of his grace.*

From these passages we learn that those *in Christ* …

- Are a **new creation.**
- Have **no condemnation.**
- Have been given **eternal life.**
- Have **salvation.**
- Find **redemption** and **forgiveness of sin.**

Salvation comes only by Jesus: *I am the way, the truth, and the life. No one comes to the Father except through Me*, John 14.6.

Paul taught that redemption is found in Christ, Romans 3.24, and would later teach that *there is no condemnation for those who are in Christ Jesus*, 8.1. There is no more important question in the world than, "How do I get to be "in Christ?"

Two New Testament passages provide the answer with abundant clarity:

- Romans 6.3: a person is *baptized **into Christ Jesus**.*
- Galatians 3.27: *For those of you who **were baptized into Christ** have been clothed with Christ.*

The pathway into Christ and thus into His church is inseparably connected to baptism. Living a secular life according to the Judeo-Christian moral code or exhibiting religious character minus Jesus is not enough. Cornelius was a good man, but still needed Christ, Acts 10.2. After teaching Jesus, Peter commanded him and his family to be baptized, Acts 10.48.

# The Essentiality of Baptism

## The Example of Christ

The synoptic gospels[27] provide the details of Jesus' baptism. John the Baptist's ministry was in full swing, preparing the way for the Messiah. When Jesus arrived from Nazareth, John first tried to discourage Him from being baptized. Matthew 3.14 says, *But John tried to stop him, saying, "I need to be baptized by you, and yet you come to me?"* Jesus responded by saying that His baptism was necessary *to fulfill all righteousness,* 3.15. The second part of the verse says that John allowed Him to be baptized.

This was a monumental moment:

- Matthew 3.16: The Holy Spirit came upon Him.
- Matthew 3.17: The Father publicly acknowledged Jesus as His Son.

For us, the occasion of our baptism is just as monumental:

- Mark 16.16: When we act in faith, baptism is the occasion we begin to experience salvation, having had our sins forgiven.
- Acts 2.38; 5.32: When we move in repentance, baptism is the occasion we receive the Holy Spirit.
- Galatians 3.26–27; Matthew 12.50: When we are baptized, we are acknowledged by God as His child.[28]

---

27  I have chosen to focus on Matthew's gospel. See also Mark 1.10–11 and Luke 3.21–22.

28  Otey, Melvin L. "Baptism and Christ." *The Gospel Advocate,* February 2015, p. 12–13.

# Apostolic Teachings: Faith, Repentance, Baptism

Before His ascension, Jesus commissioned the apostles to go into all the world and make disciples.[29] Their message of how to become a disciple involved teaching faith in Jesus as the means of salvation, repentance by turning to Christ, and baptism for salvation. Beginning with the book of Acts, the remainder of the New Testament shows the apostles in action … sharing the gospel … and including within that gospel … the essentiality of baptism:

- Acts 2.38: Peter replied, *Repent and be baptized, each of you, in the name of Jesus Christ for the forgiveness of your sins, and you will receive the gift of the Holy Spirit.*
- 1 Peter 3.21: *Baptism, which corresponds to this, now saves you (not as the removal of dirt from the body, but the pledge of a good conscience toward God) through the resurrection of Jesus Christ, …*
- Acts 22.16: *And now, why are you delaying? Get up and be baptized, and wash away your sins, calling on his name.*

## The Salvation Stories of Acts

One of the strongest cases for the essentiality of baptism is seen inside the book of Acts. Between Acts 2 and 19 we observe 10 salvation stories. Both Jew and Gentile, in many different situations and circumstances, were all presented with gospel teaching. In each account, Luke mentions differing components of how each person was led to Christ. In some cases, he includes how people heard preaching and exhortation. In the majority, he speaks of how they believed upon Christ. In Acts 2, repentance is clearly commanded. Acts 8 provides an example of the Eunuch's confession. But one thing in these stories is unmistakable and it should not go missed. Those who heard gospel teaching were baptized. It is evident as you go throughout Acts:

1. **The Jews on Pentecost, Acts 2,** listened carefully to Peter's sermon, were stirred in their heart, and asked what to do. Peter replied that they should repent and be baptized.
2. **The Samaritans, Acts 8,** *gave heed* to Philip's preaching. Both men and women were baptized.
3. **Simon, Acts 8,** believed and was baptized.

---

29  Mark 16.15–16; Luke 24.44–47.

4. **The Ethiopian, Acts 8,** confessed his faith in Jesus and was baptized at his first opportunity.
5. **Saul of Tarsus, Acts 9, 22, 26,** was baptized so that his sins would be washed away.
6. **Cornelius and all his household, Acts 10,** were baptized after receiving the Holy Spirit.
7. **Lydia and her household, Acts 16,** listened to Paul's teaching and were baptized.
8. **The Philippian jailer and his household, Acts 16,** acted upon their faith and were baptized in the middle of the night.
9. **Some Athenians, Acts 17,** *believed*. We can strongly infer they were baptized.
10. **The Corinthians, Acts 18,** heard, believed, and were baptized.
11. **The Ephesians, Acts 19,** corrected their beliefs and were baptized into Christ.

# The Mode of Baptism

Just like the essentiality of baptism is clearly communicated in Scripture, so is the mode or method of baptism. Simply put, baptism is *immersion in water*. It is not the action of dipping or pouring. Words associated with it are "plunging,"[30] "submerged," "flooded, like a submerged boat,"[31] "overwhelmed," and "to sink."[32]

Referring to Jesus' baptism, the text indicates that Jesus was immersed. John 3.23 says John was baptizing in a place where there was "plenty of water." Mark 1.10 says that Jesus and John *came up out of the water*. This same practice of going down and coming up out of a place with plenty of water is seen in how the early church carried out baptism. In Romans 6.4 and Colossians 2.12, Paul describes it as a "burial." Acts 8 also records the salvation story of the Ethiopian eunuch. Upon hearing "the good news about Jesus," he and Philip *went down into the water,* where he was baptized, 8.38.

---

30  BDAG, p. 164.

31  Moulton, James Hope, and George Milligan. *The Vocabulary of the Greek Testament.* London: Hodder and Stoughton, 1930, p. 102.

32  Abbott-Smith, G. *A Manual Greek Lexicon of the New Testament.* New York: Charles Scribner's Sons, 1922, p. 74.

The next verse specifically says *they came up out of the water.* It should be obvious that the early church practiced immersion.

## Emphasizing the Gospel ... Not Baptism

Because so many in the religious world are adamant about it not being necessary, we can become very passionate in showing how the Bible speaks of its necessity. This is certainly OK. People need to know. But we must never forget the gospel message upon which it is based.

> For Christ did not send me to baptize, but to preach the gospel—not with eloquent wisdom, so that the cross of Christ will not be emptied of its effect, 1 Corinthians 1.17.

What is Paul saying here? Obviously, he would have never talked down the importance of baptism, but his primary focus was the gospel.[33] We must aim higher. When a person has a basic understanding of his or her desperate need for God, the effects of Jesus' atoning death, and the power of God to make new, baptism at one's first opportunity will be the natural result.

Here is why I believe this is important. Over the years I have studied with both unchurched people from the world and others coming from the religious world. Some of those interactions have led to baptism, only to see the person attend worship services one time and then never return. While we need to stress the essentiality of baptism, there is more to Christianity and being right with God. We must never give off the impression that it is all that matters and once they have been baptized that they're good. If rather, we aim higher in our approach, emphasizing the gospel message and what it requires, maybe our retention rates post baptism will rise.

So, what is the gospel message?

### Defining the Gospel

"Gospel" is the good news about Jesus' life, death, and resurrection. The English word comes from *godspel,* which meant "glad tidings" or "good

---

33  Some of our religious friends who use this passage to deemphasize baptism completely miss the point of Paul's teaching. Paul was dealing with factions who were claiming special allegiance to him. His ministry wasn't about baptizing as many as he could to create his own personal following, his purpose was for the preaching of the gospel. Obviously, baptism is very much a part of the gospel message. Any other conclusion is completely ruled out by Paul's teaching in Romans 6.3–7.

news." A Greco-Roman term, it refers to a celebratory announcement, such as victory in battle or the enthronement of a king.[34] It's good news, because it provides a person an escape from the penalty of sin.

In 1 Corinthians 15, Paul outlines three important facts of the gospel:

> Now I want to make clear for you, brothers and sisters, the gospel I preached to you, which you received, on which you have taken your stand and by which you are being saved, if you hold to the message I preached to you—unless you believed in vain. For I passed on to you as most important what I also received: that Christ died for our sins according to the Scriptures, that he was buried, that he was raised on the third day according to the Scriptures, 1 Corinthians 15.1–4.

Did you catch it in the second half of v. 3 into v. 4? The gospel message **always** includes Jesus' death, burial, and resurrection. This is not just a feel-good story to *believe,* it is something that prompts us to immediate action. It must be obeyed.

In his excellent study on the gospel, David Warren argues if believing the gospel involves the central truths of Jesus' death, burial, and resurrection, so should obeying the gospel. "One must not only believe that Jesus was crucified, but a believer must also experience crucifixion."[35] *If anyone wants to follow after me, let him deny himself, take up his cross, and follow me,* Matthew 16.24. Those alive in Jesus' day would have immediately understood the graphic imagery. *Taking up a cross* meant going to your death. Coming to Christ involves the brutal death to self.

When the gospel is communicated, we are doing much more than sharing a set of steps that lead to salvation. In our teaching we must point out the devastating impact of sin.[36] We have all sinned personally against God and, on our own, have no means to remedy the situation.[37] The only solution is Jesus. The only way to life is by heeding His call. The situation is urgent because the need is real. Until one obeys the gospel call, he or she is lost. It is a monumental decision that will change the entire trajectory of a person's life.

---

34  Strauss, Mark L. *Mark*. Edited by Clinton E. Arnold. Zondervan Exegetical Commentary on the New Testament. Grand Rapids, MI: Zondervan, 2014, p. 59.

35  Warren, David H. "Set for the Defense of the Gospel." *Gospel Advocate,* February 2015, p. 16–18.

36  See Ephesians 2.1–3; 11–12.

37  See Ephesians 2.4–10.

## Death ... Then Burial ... Then Resurrection

Salvation is much more than the simple belief that Jesus died on the cross for your sins. Before someone can be brought into the kingdom, they must crucify themselves by making the decision to place Jesus in command of their life. All allegiances contrary to Christ must be severed. Going forward, His will reigns supreme and becomes *the* driving force in life.

- It is where a person begins the practice of allowing the *peace of Christ ... to rule the heart,* Colossians 3.15.
- It is when a person begins to *take every thought captive to obey Christ,* 2 Corinthians 10.5.

This is repentance ... a very personal decision to turn from self and sin to God. Another great passage that sheds light on what is involved in repentance is Galatians 5.24: *Now those who belong to Christ Jesus have crucified the flesh with its passions and desires.*

It is significant in how Paul speaks regarding the very active sense of having put something to death. It was not something done to him. He crucified himself. His death did not happen in baptism ... it preceded his burial.

Warren writes:

> Both logic and Scripture demand that death must precede the burial. Jesus first died on the cross; only then was He buried in the tomb. In a proper baptism, we do not bury a live person. We bury a person who has already died to self and to sin. ...in baptism a believer's death is joined with Christ's death just as the believer himself is joined with Christ. In baptism, a dead believer (physically still alive, but dead in regard to self and sin) enters not just Christ but also His death. At that moment, he becomes "crucified with Christ" (Galatians 2.20).[38]

Death *always* precedes burial.

Burial *always* precedes resurrection.

Many of our religious friends have been taught that baptism is an outward sign of an inward grace. They believe that it is a good thing to do, but the urgency with it is gone because they were saved and forgiven of sin at the point of faith. This belief has them thinking they are saved before baptism, which is not the way the New Testament describes salvation. Romans 6.4 however, makes it very clear that the burial in baptism happens *before* a person's resurrection to newness of life. *Therefore we were buried with him by*

---
38  Ibid, p. 17.

baptism into death, in order that, just as Christ was raised from the dead by the glory of the Father, so we too may walk in newness of life, Romans 6.4.

If a person believes they were saved before baptism … they have placed the resurrection before the burial. *How can they have obeyed the gospel?*

The order is significant. Before a person is buried, he must be dead. This happens through repentance and renunciation of self. Then and only then, is a person ready to be buried in baptism. It is only after the burial takes place that the resurrection to newness of life occurs.

## What Happens When a Person is Baptized?

1 Corinthians 6.11b describes three things that happen when we are baptized:

- We are *washed*. This is the *washing of regeneration and renewal of the Holy Spirit*, Titus 3.5. The Spirit frees us from spiritual death, cleanses us from sin, and makes us alive toward God. See also Colossians 2.13; Ephesians 2.4–5; Romans 6.3–4.
- We are *sanctified*. This is a change in position where we are moved from Satan's kingdom to God's kingdom, Colossians 1.13. Galatians 4.5–7 and Ephesians 1.5 also describe this as an adoption whereby a person becomes a member of the family of God.
- We are *justified*. This is a legal term which describes our change in status. We are declared "not guilty." See also Colossians 2.13–14.

## Baptism and the Spirit

> But when the kindness of God our Savior and his love for mankind appeared, he saved us—not by works of righteousness that we had done, but according to his mercy—through the washing of regeneration and renewal by the Holy Spirit. He poured out his Spirit on us abundantly through Jesus Christ our Savior, Titus 3.4–6.

This passage expresses the activity of God, moved by grace and mercy, who works via the Spirit to save us from eternal destruction. See how it is in baptism where we meet the Spirit for the purpose of regeneration and renewal. In that moment, the Spirit directly applies the saving benefits of Jesus' death and resurrection to us. We go from death to life.

Titus 3.4–6 helps us understand:

### Why We Were Saved

We needed to be cleansed. *Washing*, in v. 5, connects this activity with the time of baptism.[39] The only human action taking place is our personal decision, moved by repentance and sorrow for sin, to make ourselves available to God in baptism, where He performs the saving work by the Spirit. It is never *because of works done by us in righteousness, but according to His own mercy.*

### How We Were Saved

Paul says we are saved by *the washing of regeneration and renewal.* This explains what happens during your baptism. *Regeneration* comes from a word that can be translated into English as our "re-birthday." During Paul's day the word was used to talk about "coming back from death to life," or "the restoration of life of individuals."

### Who Saved You

Paul says this all happens by the Spirit, which explains **who** gave you new life. Verse 6 connects to Acts 2.38b, where Paul says that those who repent and are baptized receive the gift of the Holy Spirit.

## Conclusion

2 Thessalonians 1.7–8 describes what will happen at Jesus' second coming:

> and to give relief to you who are afflicted, along with us. This will take place at the revelation of the Lord Jesus from heaven with his powerful angels, when he takes vengeance with flaming fire on those who don't know God and on those who don't obey the gospel of our Lord Jesus.

Those who do not know God[40] as well as those who do believe in God but haven't obeyed the gospel[41] will experience the flaming fire of judgment. The

---

39 "Washing," *loutron*, refers to baptism. See also Ephesians 5.26, where it specifically refers to the washing of water. The verb form of the word is also used in Hebrews 10.22 where the writer speaks of our *bodies washed with pure water.* See Louw, Johannes P., and Eugene Albert Nida. *Greek-English Lexicon of the New Testament: Based on Semantic Domains.* New York: United Bible Societies, 1996, p. Vol. 1, p. 537.

40 This is describing those who deny the existence of God or people who have no knowledge of Him.

41 This is describing people who know about God … may believe in Him… and may

only escape from the very real reality that is forthcoming is to be *in Christ*.

In this lesson we have learned how one gets *in Christ* and thus *in His church*, which is the body of saved persons. As Peter said, *There is salvation in no one else, for there is no other name under heaven given to people by which we must be saved*, Acts 4.12.

## For Thought and Reflection

1. What blessing do the saved have by being *in Christ*?

2. What does the New Testament reveal about how to get into Christ?

3. What good things did Cornelius do? Were they enough to satisfy his need for salvation? Explain.

4. What is so monumental about Jesus' baptism? What is so monumental about ours?

5. What did the apostles teach regarding salvation?

6. What event is mentioned, in all 10 conversions stories in Acts?

7. How do we know baptism involves immersion?

---

*believe* in the gospel but have never obeyed it.

8. What is the essential message that must be communicated when we explain the need to be baptized? (1 Corinthians 15.3–4)

9. What does it mean to obey the gospel?

10. What is the order presented in Romans 6.4–6?
    _____ is followed by _____
    _____, only then can a
    _____ take place.

11. What does it mean to *crucify* your flesh?

12. Has a person who believes salvation comes before baptism obeyed the gospel? Why or why not?

13. Who do we meet in the waters of baptism? (Titus 3.4–6)

14. What three things happen in our baptism? (1 Corinthians 6.11b)

# Lesson 6

# The Role of Jesus and the Apostles in the Church

## Introduction

Our country is awash in political correctness and restraint of certain speech that has been deemed *offensive* or *intolerant*. Coupled with that is a growing disrespect of authority of any kind. In some facets of our culture outright rebellion and contempt for the government, police, parents, or anyone who traditionally holds authority over others is being championed in the media, academia, and even in households. Truly it feels as if everything is backwards. Maybe our time is growing closer to what Isaiah experienced: *Woe to those who call evil good and good evil, who substitute darkness for light and light for darkness, who substitute bitter for sweet and sweet for bitter*, Isaiah 5.20.

Christians in our country need to be careful that the world doesn't blend itself into our personal and church life. Rebellion against authority and rugged individualism is rooted into American DNA. It goes all the way back to the founding of our country. In 1776 we rebelled from England and won our independence against the tyranny of an earthly king. Now almost a quarter century in, most Americans have no idea of what it means to be a subject in a kingdom. We may fail to realize that for most of history, most humans have lived under monarchies that featured absolute control by a king or queen. What those rulers decreed was binding, often under penalty of death. There was no appeal. A person's personal rights or liberties did not matter. If a monarch ordered you to do something, you did it. Without question.

Thankfully, we serve a perfect and gracious King, who always acts in love and our best interest. Our Lord would never direct us into anything that would bring us spiritual harm or lead us away from our destination of heaven. But we also need to be aware of the authority Jesus has been given, Matthew 28.18, and that upon surrendering to Him, we go on record as allowing Him to rule our life.

In Ephesians, Paul shows us how Jesus has been given as *head over everything for the church,* Ephesians 1.22b.

This is written just after Paul expresses his great desire that Christians come to a more effective realization of the blessings they possess in Christ. Paul prays that we would come to a greater realization of *the hope of* (our) *calling,* 1.18a. He also desired that we have a better understanding of *the wealth of* (our) *glorious inheritance in the saints,* 1.18b. And finally, he intended that we experience a deeper realization of the *greatness of His power toward us who believe, according to the mighty working of His strength,* 1.19.

The same power that raised Christ from the dead, 1.20a, now resides in us. It is the same power that *seated Christ at His right hand in the heavens, far above any earthly or heavenly power,* 1.20–21. It subjected *everything under His feet,* 1.22a, and *appointed Him as head over everything for the church,* 1.22b.

Christ wasn't raised from the dead for just something ordinary. Because of Jesus' work on the cross, the Father has *highly exalted Him,* Philippians 2.9–11. At His ascension, Jesus said, *all authority* had been given to Him, Matthew 28.18. Paul makes the same case here. Jesus' victory over death and the forces of evil was a decisive triumph. The contest wasn't even close.

Now, let's read Ephesians 1.22–23 together with the context in mind. As we come to grasp the benefits of being recipients of power, God gave Jesus' victory for our benefit: *And he subjected everything under his feet and appointed him as head over everything for the church, which is his body, the fullness of the one who fills all things in every way.*

As "Head," Jesus retains all leadership and authority. As the "Head" of His church, He is also the "provider" and "supplier" of the body.[42]

> The head of the church is a victorious and powerful Lord. On this basis, Christ can impart to the church all of the empowering resources it needs to resist the attacks of powers and to engage in the mission of filling the world that God has called it to.[43]

Ephesians 1.22–23 must always be read from the standpoint of relationship. Because of the uniqueness and intimacy of His connection with those He has redeemed, He will use all His power to fulfill His purposes for us. "He

---

42  Arnold, Clinton E. *Ephesians.* Zondervan Exegetical Commentary on the New Testament. Grand Rapids, MI: Zondervan, 2010, p. 115.

43  Ibid., p. 116.

is completely over us and completely in us, our supreme Lord and supreme power."[44] The "head" and "body" metaphor is used to express the complete union the church has with Christ (similar to the imagery of the parable of the vine and the branches in John 15), the same life source flows through us all; with everything functioning in obedience to Him, carrying out His work in the world.[45]

## What Does It Mean That Jesus Is the "Head" of the Church?

When Paul says Jesus is the "head" of the church, it has profound implications for our personal morality and matters of doctrine. Jesus is King and has the power and authority to command. He is in charge. And just as our brain dictates our attitudes, words, and actions, with the body following through naturally, so does Christ with the church. The body responds appropriately inside the relationship it has with its head.

Perhaps there is no better passage that emphasizes this relationship than what Paul wrote in Colossians:

> And let the peace of Christ, to which you were also called in one body, rule your hearts. And be thankful. Let the word of Christ dwell richly among you, in all wisdom teaching and admonishing one another through psalms, hymns, and spiritual songs, singing to God with gratitude in your hearts. And whatever you do, in word or in deed, do everything in the name of the Lord Jesus, giving thanks to God the Father through him, Colossians 3.15–17.

Now, because of Jesus' work on the cross, which brought the forgiveness of sin, we are in an objective "state of peace" with our God. We have been reconciled with God, justified, or declared "not guilty."[46] In fact, earlier in Colossians Paul spoke of the peace we now have with God through Christ: *and through him to reconcile everything to himself, whether things on earth or things in heaven, by making peace through his blood, shed on the cross*, 1.20. The enmity we once had with God has been taken away, Colossians 2.14–15.

---

44 MacArthur, John F., Jr. *Ephesians*. MacArthur New Testament Commentary. Chicago: Moody Press, 1986, p. 49.

45 Foulkes, Francis. *Ephesians: An Introduction and Commentary*. Vol. 10. Tyndale New Testament Commentaries. Downers Grove, IL: InterVarsity Press, 1989, p. 73.

46 See Romans 5.1, 10–11.

Now as we focus on Colossians 3.15, we are told to let that state of peace "rule" our life. *Rule* comes from the word we use today for "umpire." Christ and the state of peace He brings is to call the shots in our life. What Christ desires reigns supreme over any of our attitudes, words, or actions. This is what Paul means when he speaks of letting that peace *rule your hearts.* Christ impacts everything. He impacts every relationship. He impacts our values. He impacts our doctrinal teaching.

Now, look at Colossians 3.17. Paul stresses that *everything* needs to be governed from the perspective of living as a subject of the risen King. When he says all our words and deeds are to be done *in the name of the Lord Jesus,* he is using his apostolic authority to command us to always act according to the nature and character of Jesus Christ. Everything we say and do must be lived out with Jesus in mind. When we were baptized into Christ, we came under His authority. We are now in union with Christ, Galatians 3.27; Romans 6.3.[47]

This has profound implications on how the church governs itself. Only Christ has the authority to legislate, James 4.12b. Therefore, there is no human law or mandate in matters of belief and practice that carry any authoritative weight. Only that which has been given by Christ and by His inspired apostles and prophets is the standard for how the church conducts itself. This also rules out our subjective feelings and experiences. Man-made church traditions are just that—*man-made*—and carry no authority with Christ.

## The Word of Christ Is the Standard

The second part of James 4.12b points out there is only one Judge. That is, of course, Jesus Christ, who uses His Word as the standard: *The one who rejects me and doesn't receive my sayings has this as his judge: The word I have spoken will judge him on the last day,* John 12.48.

There is no other standard. God's word is that by which we live. As members of His body, we simply live in unity (obedience) with His wishes. The Bible is where those wishes for godly living and correct doctrinal practices are found.

---

47   Moo, Douglas J. *The Letters to the Colossians and to Philemon.* The Pillar New Testament Commentary. Grand Rapids, MI: William B. Eerdmans Pub. Co., 2008, p. 291.

## The Authority of the Apostles

The Apostles are those who were sent out directly as authorized representatives of Jesus Christ. *As the Father has sent me, I also send to you,* John 20.21. They were taught directly by Jesus and were invested with the authority to speak on His behalf. *When the Spirit of truth comes, he will guide you into all the truth. For he will not speak on his own, but he will speak whatever he hears. He will also declare to you what is to come. He will glorify me, because he will take from what is mine and declare it to you,* John 16.13–14.

As we read through the New Testament, we learn how the teachings of the Apostles are the very word of God:

- 1 Corinthians 14.37b: … what I write to you is the Lord's command.
- 1 Thessalonians 4.15a: For we say this to you by a word from the Lord.

There are several other passages in the New Testament that explain the authority and weight of the Apostles' teaching: Acts 2.1–4; 1 Corinthians 2.4, 6–13; 11.23; 2 Corinthians 4.5–6; 5.18–20; 1 Timothy 4.1; 1 Peter 1.12; 2 Peter 3.1–2.

From the day of Pentecost on, the Apostles preached the gospel message wherever they went. Peter's sermons in Acts 2–3 and Paul's in Acts 13 and 17 are good examples of their preaching which focused on Christ's death, burial, and resurrection. Accompanying those messages was the working of supernatural signs and wonders, confirming the words they spoke were from God, Hebrews 2.1–4; 1 John 1.1–4. The foundation they established was laid down for the remainder of time: *According to God's grace that was given to me, I have laid a foundation as a skilled master builder, and another builds on it. But each one is to be careful how he builds on it. For no one can lay any foundation other than what has been laid down. That foundation is Jesus Christ,* 1 Corinthians 3.10–11.

## The Authority of New Testament Prophets

Prophets, by definition, are those who speak for another on behalf of God.[48]

---

48   **53.79 προφήτης, ου m**: one who proclaims inspired utterances on behalf of God—'prophet, inspired preacher.'[9] See Louw, Johannes P., and Eugene Albert Nida. *Greek-English Lexicon of the New Testament: Based on Semantic Domains*. New York: United Bible Societies, 1996, Vol. 1, p. 542.

In both Testamental periods, prophets spoke via inspiration.[49] The gospel has been revealed through *apostles and prophets by the Spirit,* Ephesians 3.3–6. So, when we read the inspired accounts of Mark, Luke, James, and Jude, we can know the words they wrote down carry divine authority.[50] Paul regarded Luke's gospel as authoritative when he quotes it as Scripture in 1 Timothy 5.17–18.[51]

## Conclusion

Jesus Christ is the head of His church, which is His body. He was sent by God for a very specific mission, i.e., the salvation of mankind from sin. As He worked in His earthly ministry, He appointed special men to represent Him and teach His word after His departure. The Spirit came upon these men and inspired their words and writings. Those records have been preserved for us in the Word of God. God's ways are objective and set the standard for our attitudes, words, and actions. Inside His word are specific commands and doctrinal teachings which we are expected to adopt into our life. Human traditions, subjective feelings, or claims of miraculous inspiration today are outside of what has been revealed *once and for all,* Jude 3. Therefore, those things carry no weight for us as we engage in our religious practices today.

In everything we do, let us always move with the attitude that asks, *what does the Lord say?*

---

49 Deuteronomy 18.15–22; 2 Peter 1.19–21.

50 This last section is a very condensed summary Wharton's excellent work, p. 70–71.

51 See Luke 10.7.

# For Thought and Reflection

1. In the "head" and "body" metaphor, what represented leadership and authority?

2. For whose benefit did God give Jesus victory?

3. From what perspective should Ephesians 1.22–23 always be read? Why?

4. What are some of the profound implications for Christians when we understand Jesus as "head" of the church?

5. What is the *peace* Paul mentions in Colossians 3.15? Is it a subjective feeling, or is it an objective state that we live in?

6. What does it mean that we allow *the peace of Christ* to *rule in our hearts?*

7. What does it mean that we do *everything in the name of the Lord?* (3.17)

8. What will be the standard that judges us in the last day?

9. How was the word of the Apostles to be regarded? Explain.

10. How was the work and teaching of New Testament prophets to be regarded? How did Paul regard Luke's writing?

11. With the things we've learned in this lesson being true, what does this mean for man-made doctrines, traditions, and subjective feelings and emotions when it comes to our religious practices?

# Lesson 7
# The Eldership
## Introduction

In Scripture we observe various types of leaders in action. We read about leadership in the home, of God's people, and of nations. So, it should not be surprising when we read through the New Testament and observe local church leadership: *When they had appointed elders for them in every church and prayed with fasting, they committed them to the Lord in whom they had believed*, Acts 14.23.

Going along with Luke's writing here, we also observe passages like Philippians 1.1 and Titus 1.5 that also speak of the presence of an eldership in local churches. These passages set a precedent for the New Testament church. It is expected that each local church be organized with a structure of leadership.

Congregationally, elders are an important part of what Jesus has provided for the health of the local church. Leadership plays a determining role in a congregation's maturity, direction, and peace. The decisions congregations make with whom they choose to lead can have a lasting impact … for good or bad.

The appointment of these men doesn't appear to be an option. After the establishment of a congregation, one of the most urgent matters was getting these men in place. The concept of having a permanent absence of elders was unknown. The idea of continually "working toward elders," and never getting around to appointing anyone was not entertained. The decision, over multiple generations, to just settle into navigating congregational matters via men's business meetings was unheard of. Elders were appointed *in every church*. The churches of today would do well to follow their lead.

## Elders in the New Testament Period

In the New Testament, there are three terms used for this position of leadership:

- Acts 20.17: *elder.* This word refers to someone who is older and can lead from a position of maturity, wisdom, and experience.

- Acts 20.28: *overseer*. This word describes the authoritative aspect of their role. They serve as a guide, leader, or caretaker.
- 1 Peter 5.1–2a: *shepherd*. This metaphor describes the type of relationship an elder is to have with those he serves.

We also observe four other important characteristics of the office:

1. 1 Timothy 3.2—those who served were male.
2. Philippians 1.1—the elders served in a plurality.
3. Acts 20.27—the elders were co-equal.
4. 1 Peter 5.2—their oversight was limited to the local congregation.

1 Timothy 3.1–7 and Titus 1.6–9 present us with the character traits of those who serve. This lesson is not intended to cover a point-by-point dissemination of what Paul writes in these verses. But when we take a high-level view of what Paul envisioned for the office, we find that they are men of:

- **Consistency.** In 1 Timothy 3.2, Paul uses the words *above reproach*. We might also take Titus 1.8 together with this. In both passages, Paul is speaking of behavior that characterizes a person's general pattern of life, within and without the church.
- **Self-Control.** This is a person who is not self-willed or overbearing, Titus 1.7. He is not quick tempered. He absorbs hostility and keeps cool under attack. He controls his money and his appetites, 1 Timothy 3.3. He also manages himself proactively, Titus 1.8. Discipline is the positive side of self-control.
- **Courage.** In 1 Timothy 3.2 Paul uses the word *respectable*. This is the man who has developed and displays the courage to pursue his convictions. Someone has said, he is driven by his values ... rather than by expediency. Titus 1.9 indicates that he has proven himself to handle the Word accurately, aiming for what is spiritually best for the flock he serves. Titus 1.10–13 shows how he needs to be committed to doing the will of God as he understands it, no matter what comes.

## What It Means to Be a Shepherd

*Shepherd God's flock among you, not overseeing out of compulsion but willingly, as God would have you; not out of greed for money but eagerly; not lording it over those entrusted to you, but being examples to the flock*, 1 Peter 5.2–3.

The imagery of the actions of a shepherd would have immediately been identifiable with a first century audience. Families depended on sheep for survival. Sheep provided milk, cheese, meat, clothing, and tents. Oftentimes, sheep dominated the landscape of Judea. When applied to the eldership, the metaphor of a shepherd fit perfectly in how shepherds know, care-for, feed, nurse, protect, and rescue sheep. In fact, if we wish to understand the biblical model for spiritual leadership, we can look no further than the shepherd and his flock.

In the Bible we see several persons metaphorically referred to as shepherds:

- **God, Isaiah 40.1:** Here we see the gentle, caring relationship between God and His people.
- **David, Psalm 78.70–72:** David possessed a pure heart and guided his people with skillful hands.
- **The prophets and priests of Israel, Ezekiel 34.2; 4–5:** These individuals were responsible for the spiritual well-being of the people.
- **Jesus, Ezekiel 34.23–24; Luke 15.5–6:** Our Savior left the comfort of heaven and came into our world to shepherd us.

## Shepherding Happens Inside Relationships

As we put all the pictures together, we see a shepherd as a person who is full of love, service, vulnerability, and openness. Ancient shepherds *lived* with their flock. The trust between a shepherd and his sheep began at birth and continued all the way into maturity. John 10.1–15 is a great passage where Jesus speaks about shepherding and how He is the Great Shepherd. Each individual sheep knew the shepherd's voice and his alone. They relied on him. They followed him and no one else. Every night the shepherds would lead their flock into a fold, where he would serve as their protection from any and every predator. Through the shared experience of life, shepherds built and nurtured enduring and trusting relationships with their flock.

What can we learn from this?

Shepherds who serve local congregations today need to exhibit hands-on and personal involvement with the flock. They are not CEO's who bark out orders from a distance … they are right there in the middle of life with those they serve. They exhibit:

## Accessibility

Shepherds must be committed to knowing the members of their congregation. This involves time spent outside of the church building. They need to be accessible ... and each member needs to feel that so they can receive the proper help and attention when trouble comes.

## Commitment

Shepherds must be committed to the time and effort required to build open and authentic relationships ... all of which is done with a view of the long-term. There is no better example to consider than Jesus, who, for almost three years, spent His life *with* the apostles.[52] Jesus taught them, ate with them, rested with them, and protected them. His influence on them was so great that other people could tell they had been around Jesus: *When they observed the boldness of Peter and John and realized that they were uneducated and untrained men, they were amazed and recognized that they had been with Jesus*, Acts 4.13.

## Trust

Trust is not gained in an instant, but rather it is built over time. It comes when the shepherd invests his life in the lives of the sheep. It's personal.

> Truly I tell you, anyone who doesn't enter the sheep pen by the gate but climbs in some other way is a thief and a robber. The one who enters by the gate is the shepherd of the sheep. The gatekeeper opens it for him, and the sheep hear his voice. He calls his own sheep by name and leads them out. When he has brought all his own outside, he goes ahead of them. The sheep follow him because they know his voice. They will never follow a stranger; instead they will run away from him, because they don't know the voice of strangers, John 10.1–5.

Did you catch what Jesus said? *He calls his own sheep by name and leads them out. ... The sheep follow him because they know his voice.* It's personal. Jesus knows us by name. So, it should be with the shepherd who serves the local flock. They know our names and personal stories.

Everything about shepherding goes back to relationships. Relationships are built on accessibility, commitment, and trust.

---

52  See Mark 3.14. The apostles went everywhere Jesus went. We see them attending weddings, funerals, and worship together.

# Elders and Congregations Have Responsibilities to Each Other

Any relationship involves mutual responsibilities. Shepherds will never serve effectively unless those they serve understand their own obligations to their leaders.

## 1 Thessalonians 5.12—We Must Appreciate Our Shepherds

Members of the congregation need to become well acquainted with those who serve them. In fact, the relationship should grow to where a person feels comfortable to go to them at any time with *any* personal problem. When we know our shepherds well, it removes the awkwardness that may come when we go to them with a pressing need. We need to know them and interact with them not just during times of difficulty. Paul urged the Thessalonians to *give recognition to* their spiritual leaders. Because of their dedication and sacrifice, their leadership should be cherished and appreciated.

## 1 Thessalonians 5.13—We Must Regard Them Very Highly in Love

There is no higher honor bestowed upon a man than that of a shepherd. He is a person who has been entrusted with the care of individual souls inside the church. That responsibility alone should make him worthy of honor and respect. Theirs is an office of dignity. It is also an office of authority. As they guide us, we need to regard their instruction with a sense of seriousness.

We should also regard them with a loving spirit. They are not perfect men. They make mistakes. They are always working to grow in patience. Our relationship with them was never intended to be adversarial. We should always respond with love and grace. Nothing matters unless it is done in love, 1 Corinthians 13.4–7. If people inside our congregations were more deeply committed to the principles of 1 Thessalonians 5.12–13, there would be much more harmony and cooperation with the eldership.

## Hebrews 13.17—We Must Submit to Their Judgment

In the church, Jesus is the Lawgiver, James 4.12. No person has the right make up, delete, or alter any of Christ's commandments. In their work, our overseers have been tasked to carry out the commands. However, there are many other matters of judgment that they do have rule over. In those matters, this passage from Hebrews teaches us to allow their decisions to prevail over ours. The wording in the original language instructs us to have the type of spirit that will yield to their authority and possess an attitude that desires to obey.[53]

What is said next in this verse must not go unnoticed. Our shepherds *keep watch over (our) souls as those who will give an account.* We must not neglect the tremendous responsibility placed on the shoulders of an elder. They work to ensure every soul in the local congregation gets to heaven. There will be times where every member inside the local congregation will need the spiritual help and assistance of their shepherds. Many situations they handle are not easy. They often see hours of the night the rest of us do not as they wrestle over how best to help with the problems others face. There are many sleepless nights as they pray, weep, and find themselves in the trenches with those they are trying to help work through a problem.

It is never fun to sit down with a member and admonish, rebuke, or correct them in some way. We must always remember their love, care, and desire for our success. Always remember, they watch over your soul.

## Hebrews 13.7—We Must Imitate Our Elders

We need to be mindful of their instruction in righteousness, their personal counsel and example. Just as they are faithful to the Word, so should we be. It is easy to take our leaders for granted. It is also easy to criticize our leaders. What if less time were spent in criticism and instead, we devoted our time looking for the good to imitate? How would that change our congregations? If we fail to imitate their righteous faith, we have missed the mark.

## What Do Elders Really Do?

A former shepherd looked back on his time of service to a local congregation and reflected on what the work was like while he served. These provide great insight into what it is like to be a shepherd:

- We love God and appreciate the hope he has given and demonstrate that as best we can by being an example, providing spiritual guidance, and teaching.

---

53    BDAG, p. 1030.

- We plan for ways to increase each member's understanding of God's Word. We set up Bible studies with members in mind, and we have a vision of Heaven we want to share.
- We view the local church as our family, and at times it requires correction out of love for the eternal souls of our members.
- We keep open doors to listen to our brothers and sisters and bear their burdens. We pray continually for God's guidance and the wisdom supplied by the Spirit to lead us in the right direction.
- We sacrifice our time and energy to focus on the spiritual wellbeing of those we are charged to oversee.
- We are careful to act without being willful, but also realize the need to serve as ministers of God in directing the local congregation.
- Elders grow in their understanding that all their time belongs to the Lord for the purpose of leading His faithful to heaven. Our work is out of dedication to the Lord and our love of souls. Our pay is to serve God and hear Him say "Well done." We have no greater call than to see the Lord in heaven and live eternally in His presence.

## Conclusion

The importance of a local congregation having qualified, humble leaders who love the Lord and His word cannot be under-emphasized. No work is greater and more effective. No work is more vital to the local church.

*If anyone aspires to be an overseer, he desires a noble work,* 1 Timothy 3.1.

## For Thought and Reflection

1. What is the Holy Spirit's expectation regarding the presence of leadership inside the local church?

2. What is wrong with a congregation continually settling for church organization without elders?

3.  What are the three terms used to describe the leadership position of an elder? What do they each mean?

4.  How does 1 Timothy 3.2 and Titus 1.8 demonstrate the principle of consistency when it comes to biblical leaders?

5.  Do these principles imply perfection in any way? Explain.

6.  Why is self-control so important for the leader? In 1 Timothy 3 and Titus 1 how does Paul present this from both negatives and positives?

7.  What does it mean to be driven by values rather than expediency? Why is this important as we think about our leaders?

8.  How vital were shepherds to the first century world? What imagery would have been created in the minds of those inside the early church as they examined these teachings?

9.  Shepherds and their flocks lived their life together. What can we learn from this as we think of church leadership today?

10. What does it mean to be accessible?

11. What type of relationship should the shepherd intend to build with those in the local church? Why is this so important?

# Lesson 8

# Deacons and Evangelists

## Introduction

We read of **deacons** in Philippians 1.1 and 1 Timothy 3.8–13. In both passages they are brought up just after the mentioning of elders. Separate and distinct from the eldership, deacons played a special role in the New Testament church. They were servants tasked by the overseers to attend to specific tasks and needs within the congregation. They were to be serious about their example and proven men of character. Their work and dedication to God would not have been a mystery to those they served. Theirs is a position of service.

**Evangelists** are mentioned by Paul in Ephesians 4.11–12. Here they are listed as an essential part of the local congregation. They, along with elders and teachers *equip members for the work of service.* They are *bringers of good news* by helping spread the gospel. Theirs, like deacons, is an integral part of the work of the local church. Theirs is also a position of service.

This lesson will present a short overview of the work of deacons and evangelists.

## Deacons

Today, the word we use for "deacon" comes from a word that, in the original language, meant *servant*. Other words associated with it are *minister, waiter, or attendant.* They are a person who executes the commands of others. Theirs is a role separate from the eldership. Deacons do not hold any authority in the church but serve very important roles in holding responsibility over the physical needs of the congregation. Serving as a deacon always involves work. They are fundamental to church work and growth. If deacons are not busy working and serving, then it is likely the congregation is not working and growing.

Good leadership and proper teaching/communication by the shepherds will keep a congregation from having evangelists do the work of elders, elders doing the work of deacons, and the deacons doing nothing. In this scenario, Satan wins. In some places, *elders are the best deacons a congregation can have.*

This is not what God designed. Elders are to devote their work to prayer, spiritual ministry, and care of the saints. When deacons are vigorous in their work, the congregation will be alive, growing, and full of life.

## Character Traits Required

Paul was very concerned that the right *type* of person be appointed to church offices. So, by way of the Spirit, he includes a listing of character traits and lifestyle habits that need to be examined for each person who desires the role.

> Deacons, likewise, should be worthy of respect, not hypocritical, not drinking a lot of wine, not greedy for money, holding the mystery of the faith with a clear conscience. They must also be tested first; if they prove blameless, then they can serve as deacons. Wives, likewise, should be worthy of respect, not slanderers, self-controlled, faithful in everything. Deacons are to be husbands of one wife, managing their children and their own households competently. For those who have served well as deacons acquire a good standing for themselves and great boldness in the faith that is in Christ Jesus, 1 Timothy 3.8–13.

These verses can be summarized in three ways. A deacon must:

1. Possess integrity in personal character.
2. Be building a strong spiritual life.
3. Have a good family life.

## What Their Work is Not

### Teaching

While deacons can certainly teach, their work is not a teaching office. During the first century, it appears they were directed by the overseers for specific physical tasks, seeing to the material needs of the congregation.

### A Check on the Elders

A deacon must not view himself as part of a secondary group of overseers. They are not in place to provide a system of checks and balances for the elders. Rather, they are subordinate to them. They complement the work the shepherds are doing. While the shepherds have liberty to perform all the functions of deacons, deacons cannot perform all the functions of shepherds. Therefore, deacons are not independent of the leadership oversight of the shepherds.

## What Their Work Is
### A Life of Ministry

Serving as a deacon involves an attitude and life dedicated to service and ministry. This is best exemplified in Acts 6. The men we read of here were not deacons. They were simply servants who were selected by the congregation for a specific set of tasks. The requirements were simple. They needed to be honest men who were fully committed to spiritual things. They needed to be demonstrating wisdom. They needed to love the church.

### Selfless Service

The book of Acts gives us a great example of a person who faithfully demonstrated what it means to be a servant: Philip the evangelist. He is first mentioned in Acts 6 as one of the seven men chosen to minister to the Hellenistic widows who had been neglected in the daily serving. We see him next in Acts 8 where he is in Samaria teaching and preaching. He was a man free of prejudice and was fully convinced of the need to take the gospel to *everyone*. It would have been quite an experience for any native-born Jew to travel to such an area to preach. But there was a need there, so he went. Acts 8.5–8 says many people responded to the gospel call. Philip was willing to go wherever God wanted him to go and be whatever God wanted him to be.

Later we see Philip in Acts 21.8–14. Paul visited his house during his return to Jerusalem. This visit had all the potential of being awkward at best. You may remember Paul participated in the stoning of Stephen, another one of the original "seven" of Acts 6. Philip might have even been there the day Stephen died. Now, Philip is hosting the man who participated in the killing of his friend. But, because Philip is a servant … and knows of Paul's repentance and salvation, he welcomed him into his home. When Agabus warned of Paul's impending persecution, Acts 21.11, tears were shed. No doubt Philip would have been part of this group. This is a tremendous example of a servant's heart.

## Evangelists

The word only appearing three times in the New Testament (Acts 21.8; Ephesians 4.11; 2 Timothy 4.5), an *evangelist* is a proclaimer of the gospel.[54]

---

54  Arndt, William, Frederick W. Danker, Walter Bauer, and F. Wilbur Gingrich. *A Greek-English Lexicon of the New Testament and Other Early Christian Literature*. Chicago:

One place where *evangelist* is used is found in Ephesians 4.11–12 where they are part of the group of servants given to the church: *And he himself gave some to be apostles, some prophets, some evangelists, some pastors and teachers, to equip the saints for the work of ministry, to build up the body of Christ.*

While Timothy stayed in many places for various lengths of time, his ministry was one on the move. He often traveled from place to place preaching the gospel. As we read in the previous section, Philip the *evangelist* traveled to Samaria as well as remote desert regions to preach the gospel, Acts 8. As he went along, he preached Christ, Acts 8.5. His purpose was to win people over with the gospel message: *the people were all paying attention to what Philip said*, Acts 8.6a. Later in the chapter we read of him preaching Jesus to the Ethiopian eunuch, Acts 8.35. The chapter concludes with Philip's activity after the eunuch was converted: *Philip appeared in Azotus, and he was traveling and preaching the gospel in all the towns until he came to Caesarea*, Acts 8.40.

Philip serves as a good example of preaching the gospel in new areas, where the gospel hasn't gone before, and planting a church. Timothy is an illustration of a man who went where congregations were already established and urged them to take the gospel to their city. In 2 Timothy 4.5, Timothy is instructed to *do the work of an evangelist.* This is primarily the task of preaching the gospel. His task was also to help grow congregations to maturity through the work of teaching and exhortation.

- 1 Timothy 4.6: *If you point these things out to the brothers and sisters, you will be a good servant of Christ Jesus, nourished by the words of the faith and the good teaching that you have followed.* An evangelist helps nourish people in faith and teaching.
- 1 Timothy 4.13: *Until I come, give your attention to public reading, exhortation, and teaching.* This is the evangelist's part in leading a congregation to maturity. In vv. 15–16, Paul will tell Timothy to pay attention to his teaching or doctrine so that he could be an effective teacher ... leading the congregation to maturity. This takes time, often years of work.
- 2 Timothy 2.2: *What you have heard from me in the presence of many witnesses, commit to faithful men who will be able to teach others also.* The evangelist trains up other people to teach and share the good news.

---

University of Chicago Press, 2000, p. 403.

- Titus 1.5: *The reason I left you in Crete was to set right what was left undone and, as I directed you, to appoint elders in every town.* Evangelists appointed elders.

Going back to Ephesians 4.11–12, evangelists have been given to the church for the purpose of equipping saints for the work of ministry. In other words, he plays a key role in helping lead saints to maturity, Ephesians 4.13. His work should not go unappreciated.

## Conclusion

Like the eldership, evangelists and deacons are first and foremost, servants. Unlike the eldership, their roles do not carry any authority over the congregation. However, their essentiality and spiritual influence on others needs to be appreciated and respected. They are to be spiritual men who have fully dedicated themselves to the work of the Lord. They need to love people and love Jesus Christ even more.

## For Thought and Reflection

1. What would be a simple definition of a deacon? Could you summarize it in one word? What would that be?

2. How are deacons the key to church work and growth? What happens when the deacons are not performing their function as they should?

3. What are the three basic categories of living that characterize who a deacon should be?

4. Before a deacon is appointed, what should be evident in his life? (1 Timothy 3.10a)

5. How do deacons complement the work of elders?

6. How does Philip serve as a great example of a deacon?

7. What is an evangelist? What three passages are evangelists mentioned in the New Testament?

8. How does Paul explain the purpose of their role in Ephesians 4.11–12?

9. What can we learn about the work of an evangelist from Philip?

10. What can we learn about the work of an evangelist from Timothy?

11. Were evangelists simply itinerant preachers who constantly moved around? Or did they stay awhile at a place and help the congregation to maturity? Or do we see them doing both? Explain.

12. What were some of the things Paul expected Timothy to do as an evangelist?

13. What was the evangelist Titus charged to do?

# Lesson 9

# The Heart Behind Giving

## Introduction

Giving is the channel to blessing: *Give, and it will be given to you; a good measure—pressed down, shaken together, and running over—will be poured into your lap. For with the measure you use, it will be measured back to you*, Luke 6.38.

Modern audiences may miss the imagery in this verse. Most Jews wore long robes that extended to their feet and would wear a belt around their waist. The bottom portion of the robe could be pulled up above the belt and be formed into a large pocket for things to be carried. This is what Jesus is referring to when He says the blessings will be *poured into your lap*. The garment would literally be filled with grain.[55] The point that Jesus is trying to make is that God wants to fill our laps with abundant blessings to the point where they overflow.

Giving brings us reward from God. If you want blessing from God, if you want it poured out, overflowing, pressed down, shaken together, and running over, then give. You give and He gives back more.

Perhaps this is why Paul quotes Jesus, who said, *it is more blessed to give than receive*, Acts 20.35. What you give always brings you greater blessing than what you receive.

How much do we believe these promises? How easy is it to operate from the perspective of protecting everything and holding on to it? For some, self-preservation has led to stinginess. Will we operate by only what we can see, or will we move in faith and trust in God?

Just before Paul closes his letter to the Philippians he writes out an incredible promise: *And my God will supply all your needs according to his riches in glory in Christ Jesus*, Philippians 4.19. God will meet every need. Because of Him, we have some security in the promise of tomorrow. God will meet *every* need. We have nothing to fear for tomorrow. This is a foundational principle for the Christian life, and it should have a tremendous impact on our giving.

---

55  We also see this practice in Ruth 3.15.

Will we trust in God's promise?

But there is more. This is also a matter of obedience. Going back to our text in Luke 6.38, Jesus issues a command: *Give.* So, *not giving* is sin. It is a sin against God because of a lack of trust. It is a sin against God because of a lack of obedience.

In and of themselves, Luke 6.38 and Acts 20.35 should be enough to create the type of response needed to influence us to give generously, unselfishly, and sacrificially.

## The Early Church Was a Giving Church

Reading through the New Testament we observe:

### Christians Supported Their Leaders

The early church supported apostles, evangelists, prophets, and elders because they were charged with serving and working for the church. In 1 Corinthians 9 Paul is referencing his own ministry when he writes:

> Or do only Barnabas and I have no right to refrain from working? Who serves as a soldier at his own expense? Who plants a vineyard and does not eat its fruit? Or who shepherds a flock and does not drink the milk from the flock? Am I saying this from a human perspective? Doesn't the law also say the same thing? For it is written in the law of Moses, Do not muzzle an ox while it treads out grain. Is God really concerned about oxen? Isn't he really saying it for our sake? Yes, this is written for our sake, because he who plows ought to plow in hope, and he who threshes should thresh in hope of sharing the crop. If we have sown spiritual things for you, is it too much if we reap material benefits from you? 1 Corinthians 9.6–11.

Soldiers serve the government, and the government pays them. Those who plant a garden eat from it. The ox is fed for his plowing. Likewise, those who work and serve the church should be supported by the church. There are two other passages written by Paul after this that are very direct:

- 1 Corinthians 9.14: *In the same way, the Lord has commanded that those who preach the gospel should earn their living by the gospel.*
- Galatians 6.6: *Let the one who is taught the word share all his good things with the teacher.*
- 1 Timothy 5.17: *The elders who are good leaders are to be considered worthy of double honor, especially those who work hard at preaching and teaching.*

All these passages leave us with the example of providing ongoing support for the elders, ministers, and other servants of the church.

## Christians Met the Needs of People

Benevolent needs were always present inside the early church. Widows, orphans, and poor people had needs that had to be met. Those who had been blessed with resources were instructed to share and thus store up treasure in heaven:

> Instruct those who are rich in the present age not to be arrogant or to set their hope on the uncertainty of wealth, but on God, who richly provides us with all things to enjoy. Instruct them to do what is good, to be rich in good works, to be generous and willing to share, storing up treasure for themselves as a good foundation for the coming age, so that they may take hold of what is truly life, 1 Timothy 6.17–19.

There were great needs to share … then … and now. Many among us have needs. God calls upon us to share. The principle is found throughout Scripture:

> "If there is a poor person among you, one of your brothers within any of your city gates in the land the Lord your God is giving you, do not be hardhearted or tightfisted toward your poor brother. Instead, you are to open your hand to him and freely loan him enough for whatever need he has. Be careful that there isn't this wicked thought in your heart, 'The seventh year, the year of canceling debts, is near,' and you are stingy toward your poor brother and give him nothing. He will cry out to the Lord against you, and you will be guilty. Give to him, and don't have a stingy heart when you give, and because of this the Lord your God will bless you in all your work and in everything you do. For there will never cease to be poor people in the land; that is why I am commanding you, 'Open your hand willingly to your poor and needy brother in your land,' Deuteronomy 15.7–11.

Note the directive Israel had concerning the care of other poor Israelites:

- They were not to be hardhearted or *tightfisted.*
- They were to open their hand to him and *freely loan him enough for whatever need he has.*
- When you give, the Lord will *bless you in all your work and in everything you do.*

Give and God will bless. The Psalmist wrote:

> Happy is one who is considerate of the poor; the Lord will save him in a day of adversity. The Lord will keep him and preserve him; he will be blessed in

the land. You will not give him over to the desire of his enemies. The LORD will sustain him on his sickbed; you will heal him on the bed where he lies, Psalm 41.1–3.

You should also take the time to discover the principles in Proverbs 14.31; 19.17; 22.2, 9.

### A Greater Motive

When we see the early church giving to meet the needs of the poor, it wasn't just out of meeting someone's need … it was to be generated by genuine love and concern. We must not forget the tremendous racial hatred and animosity of the first century. (Ours is not the only era of racial tension and hatred.) The hostility between Jew and Gentile must not be forgotten. Overcoming it was a serious concern. When those in the church helped others, no matter what race or background they were, it was an expression of love and spiritual unity.

## 2 Corinthians 8: Giving is the Behavior of Dedicated Christians

### 2 Corinthians 8.1–8—The Example of the Church in Macedonia

The Jerusalem church had fallen on hard times. Once a rich church, see Acts 2.42–47 and 4.32–37, now they were beset by poverty, brought on by persecution and famine. The Macedonian churches became a wonderful example of giving to meet the needs of the church in Jerusalem. What is notable about these churches is that they were impoverished themselves. They were profoundly poor. Yet *in their extreme poverty* they *overflowed in a wealth of generosity on their part*, 2 Corinthians 8.1–3.

### 2 Corinthians 8.9 – When We Give, We Are Being Like Jesus

*For you know the grace of our Lord Jesus Christ: Though he was rich, for your sake he became poor, so that by his poverty you might become rich,* 2 Corinthians 8.9. Paul has just written about the generosity of the Macedonians and now he turns attention to Jesus, the greatest example of giving. The gift Jesus brought has made us infinitely rich.

## 2 Corinthians 8.10–12—Giving is the Desire of the Converted Heart

> And in this matter I am giving advice because it is profitable for you, who began last year not only to do something but also to want to do it. Now also finish the task, so that just as there was an eager desire, there may also be a completion, according to what you have. For if the eagerness is there, the gift is acceptable according to what a person has, not according to what he does not have, 2 Corinthians 8.10–12.

Giving is commanded. Giving is important. But, as for the amount, that is left up to the giver. Giving is something that we should desire to do, and it should be something that arises from the heart. It is never a matter of manipulation or intimidation. It is the desire to bless others. It is done in proportion to what one has. It is to be done with eagerness.

## 2 Corinthians 8.13–15—Giving is the Compassionate Response to Need

> It is not that there should be relief for others and hardship for you, but it is a question of equality. At the present time your surplus is available for their need, so that their abundance may in turn meet your need, in order that there may be equality. As it is written: The person who had much did not have too much, and the person who had little did not have too little, 2 Corinthians 8.13–15.

We do not give to make ourselves poor so that others may become rich. We give so that there may be balance. Presently, you may have a surplus. But one day you might not. Give to those in need so that you might be blessed when you have need. It's all done out of compassion.

## 2 Corinthians 8.16–21—Giving is Honorable before God and Men

*Indeed, we are giving careful thought to do what is right, not only before the Lord but also before people,* 2 Corinthians 8.21. Paul had regard for what is honorable, not only in the sight of God, but also of men. While our first responsibility is to be pleasing to God, we do not live in a vacuum. Others outside the church are also watching. How do they see our generosity? Do we back up our profession with action?

## 2 Corinthians 8.22–24—Giving is the Proof of Love

*Therefore, show them proof before the churches of your love and of our boasting about you,* 2 Corinthians 8.24. When we give, we demonstrate the proof of our love for others. It is the following of Jesus' command: *A new commandment I give to you, that you love one another, even as I have loved you, that you also love one another. By this all men will know that you are my disciples, if you have love for one another,* John 13.34–35. A loving church is a generous church.

## For Thought and Reflection

1. Read Luke 6.38. Is giving a suggestion or a command? In this verse, what is the promise connected to giving?

2. What is the point of Paul's teaching in Acts 20.35?

3. For what two purposes did the early church give?

4. How did the churches in Macedonia set an example in giving?

5. What motivated the Macedonians to give so abundantly?

6. How has Jesus set the example in giving?

7. Why should the Christian be so eager to give?

8. How is giving an act of compassion?

9. How can our giving reflect positively on the church?

10. How would John 13.34–35 connect with the principle of our giving?

# Lesson 10
# The Work of the Lord's People
## Introduction

As God's people organize and work in a collective manner, what is our role and purpose? Many confusing voices have loudly spoken over the past few generations. Does the church exist to promote political agendas that legislate morality? Is the church merely a community action organization that is known more for the services it provides rather than a soul saving body of believers? What exactly are God's people to be known for?

In this lesson we will discuss the role God's people play in our world today.

## Sharing the Gospel

At the conclusion of Matthew and Mark we read of Jesus' great commission. Matthew records:

> Jesus came near and said to them, "All authority has been given to me in heaven and on earth. Go, therefore, and make disciples of all nations, baptizing them in the name of the Father and of the Son and of the Holy Spirit, teaching them to observe everything I have commanded you. And remember, I am with you always, to the end of the age." (Matthew 28.18–20)

This is not a suggestion or a wish. It is a command. It is the mission. It is to be what we are known for. The early church followed through and so must we. Luke writes about their mission focus in Acts 5.42: *Every day in the temple, and in various homes, they continued teaching and proclaiming the good news that Jesus is the Messiah.*

What are we proclaiming? Does the world know more about our favorite sports teams, hobbies, or politics than our love for the Lord? What fills our social media feeds? If you reviewed all your posts over the last three months, what topics would dominate? How much are you focused on the mission?

## It's about the Lost, Not about People Being Wrong

As we focus on the mission, it is very important to maintain the proper perspective. How do we look at the world and what we are trying to accomplish? Our job is to offer spiritual solutions through the gospel that transforms people and changes their lives. Again, note that Christians offer solutions … not judgment.

In his preaching, Ken Weliever[56] references John Fisher who wrote a piece called "Lost and Found." Fisher writes, "The world is not wrong as much as it is lost. 'Lost" is the operative word. For some time in church circles, it seems to have been very important to emphasize that the world is wrong." This, Fisher argues, has produced a mixed message that says, "We love you and we want you to know Christ died for your sins, but we really don't like you unless you think the way we do." It would be much better if we decided not to think so much of the world as being wrong as it is lost. "Someone coming to my rescue is a much better sight than someone coming to be my judge," says Fisher.

This is the spirit of Jesus, who as He taught in the synagogues, preaching the good news of the kingdom, *He felt compassion for them, because they were distressed and dejected, like sheep without a shepherd,* Matthew 9.36. May we adopt this same perspective as we reach out to our world.

## Show Our Connection to God through Worship

While there is an aspect of our life where we worship God every day through the offering of our life as a spiritual sacrifice, Romans 12.1, Christians have been assembling on the first day of the week since the establishment of the church. Passages like Acts 20.7 and others show it was their habit to be together to worship God.

### Why We Worship

The opening verses of Psalm 95 detail some important details that show our motivation to come together and sing praise, engage the Father in prayer, and bow down in worship.

- Psalm 95.1–2—*God is our rock.* He is our salvation. This fact alone should produce joy.
- Psalm 95.3—*God is a great God,* the King above all Gods.
- Psalm 95.4–5—*God is the Creator of the world.* The world belongs to Him. He is in control. The mountains are His.

---

56  Weliever, Ken. "The Role of the Church in Society." Preached 06/22/2021, Cornerstone Church of Christ, Centerville, OH. Online: Cornerstone Church of Christ - Classes & Sermons (cornerstone-coc.com)

- Psalm 95.6—*God is our Creator.* He made you. He made every person.
- Psalm 95.7—*God is our Shepherd.* He is our protector.

As you read Psalm 95.1–7, please notice the vertical focus and direction of our worship. We are there to praise, adore, and reverence God. While we may be moved by the horizontal aspects of that worship, we must remember those feelings are *the result* of our connection with God, not the *aim* of why we come together.

### Worship Presents an Opportunity

Our collective worship assembly every Sunday allows us to pour out our hearts to God in praise and prayer together with other Christians. It displays our connection with God. For guests who visit our assembly, this is a powerful message. We declare our dependence upon Him. We express the warmth of our love. We recognize His guiding hand in our past, celebrate His powerful relationship in our present, and proclaim our rock-solid trust in the future when we remember Jesus' death in communion and thereby declare, *He's coming back,* Matthew 26.29; 1 Corinthians 11.26.

For those in the world who are lonely, searching, and in need of a connection with God and His people, our worship assembly makes a strong statement about who God is, how He is approached, and how we connect with Him together with other Christians.

## Demonstrate Christian Discipleship

In Ephesians 4, Paul speaks of gifts God has provided for His church. He has given us *evangelists, pastors,* and *teachers* for the equipping of saints, *for the work of ministry* and the *building up* of *the body of Christ,* 4.11–12. This *equipping* is nothing more than discipleship training where day by day we are all becoming more and more like Jesus. Just before this, in Ephesians 2.8–10, Paul said that we have been saved by grace through faith for the purpose of displaying the incredible workmanship of God. We are His *masterpiece.* Day by day through our good works, *which God prepared beforehand,* we display God's power to change lives through our changed lifestyle.

How you live matters. Peter spoke of our new identity in 1 Peter 2.9–10. We are a *chosen race, a royal priesthood, a holy nation,* and *a people for his possession.* These descriptions are all to help us understand our newfound purpose in Christ. Together the church, God's called out people, *proclaim the praises of the one who called (us) out of darkness into His marvelous light*. We are to live *as strangers and exiles* and *conduct ourselves honorably …so they will observe your good works and glorify God on the day he visits*, 2.11–12. People are watching. Nothing is more detrimental to the cause of Christ when our practice does not match our profession.

Therefore, the church is committed to admonishing (warning one another), Romans 15.14. When members fall short, they confess their sins to one another, James 5.16. Each member of the church is committed to others … in fact we bear one another's burdens, Galatians 6.2. Each member of the body is committed to the work of exhorting each other, Hebrews 3.13; 1 Thessalonians 5.11.

## Exhibit the Closeness of the Christian Community

One of the most beautiful descriptions of the early church is found in Acts 2.42–47:

> They devoted themselves to the apostles' teaching, to the fellowship, to the breaking of bread, and to prayer. Everyone was filled with awe, and many wonders and signs were being performed through the apostles. Now all the believers were together and held all things in common. They sold their possessions and property and distributed the proceeds to all, as any had need. Every day they devoted themselves to meeting together in the temple, and broke bread from house to house. They ate their food with joyful and sincere hearts, praising God and enjoying the favor of all the people. Every day the Lord added to their number those who were being saved.

Did you catch all the key words in this text? These are certainly worth highlighting:

- Fellowship
- The believers were together
- They held all things in common
- They ate their meals together
- They praised God
- They enjoyed the favor of all the people

Those in the early church understood that their relationship with Christ brought with it a certain sense of responsibility to each other. Their sharing together was not just during their formal gatherings. It also involved the entire course of their life, i.e., financial contributions, table fellowship, and general friendship and unity characterized the early church on a day-to-day basis.⁵⁷ All of this was to express and cultivate their love for one another.

This, of course, is the application of John 13.34–35:

> "I give you a new command: Love one another. Just as I have loved you, you are also to love one another. By this everyone will know that you are my disciples, if you love one another."

Our closeness and sacrificial love for one another is the product of our relationship with Jesus Christ. It is what makes for the warm greetings and expressions of love when we are in each other's presence, 1 Corinthians 16.20; 2 Corinthians 13.12. It is heard and felt in the songs we sing to one another, 1 Corinthians 14.26; Ephesians 5.19. It is seen through heartfelt corporate and personal prayer for one another, Acts 2.42; 12.5. It is observed when Christians use their spiritual gifts and talents in service to one another, 1 Peter 4.10. It is also seen in the sharing of each other's financial needs; Acts 4.32–37; 1 Corinthians 16.1–2. And finally, the closeness of our community is seen by the way we comfort each other during the difficulties of life, 1 Thessalonians 4.16.

## To Demonstrate the Compassion of Christ through Service

The world needs to feel our compassion. We love others the way Jesus loves us. This is not just a profession; our love is filled with action and can be seen by our kind, comforting, and encouraging words and deeds. Christ identified those who follow Him as *light:*

> "You are the light of the world. A city situated on a hill cannot be hidden. No one lights a lamp and puts it under a basket, but rather on a lampstand, and it gives light for all who are in the house. In the same way, let your light shine before others, so that they may see your good works and give glory to your Father in heaven, Matthew 5.14–16.

We shine for the glory of God. In doing this we show the way to Jesus. He has saved us to serve.

- **Galatians 6.9–10:** Let us not get tired of doing good, for we will reap at the proper time if we don't give up. Therefore, as we have opportunity, let us work for the good of all, especially for those who belong to the

---

57  Seccombe, *Possessions*, 204. Cf. D. G. Peterson, *Engaging with God: A Biblical Theology of Worship* (Leicester: Apollos; Grand Rapids: Eerdmans, 1992), 153–55.

household of faith.
- **Matthew 7.12:** Therefore, whatever you want others to do for you, do also the same for them, for this is the Law and the Prophets.
- **Matthew 22.39–40:** The second is like it: Love your neighbor as yourself. All the Law and the Prophets depend on these two commands.

Do people see our service and ministry?

## For Thought and Reflection

1. What is Jesus' expectation regarding the sharing of the gospel? Is it optional?

2. What message is the church to proclaim? What are some ways we can get off track with this?

3. Why would it be more effective not to think of the world as being wrong as it is lost?

4. Why do we worship God? What direction and focus should our worship be?

5. With what opportunity does worship present us with?

6. What kind of impact does our work and discipleship make on many of the lost we communicate with?

7. What is Christian fellowship?

8. Was fellowship something just engaged in inside the place of assembly?

9. What is the natural result of a relationship with Jesus? (John 13.34–35)

10. What are some things you can do to let others see our service and ministry?

# Lesson 11
# The Reverence of Worship

## Introduction

We always need to challenge ourselves with a deeper understanding of who God is. It is important to reverence God in worship and develop a deeper appreciation of His holiness. If we can better understand who God is and how holy He is, it will go far in helping us create a spirit of reverence in worship.

Who is God? How can mere humans even come close to grasping an infinite God? How can we have a full understanding of immortality? While we have been given a measure of intelligence, it will never compare with the knowledge of God. *God's foolishness is wiser than human wisdom, and God's weakness is stronger than human strength*, 1 Corinthian 1.25. There has only been so much revealed to us. This is why we are left to trust in God more than we can explain about Him.

God wants us to trust and obey:

> Trust in the LORD with all your heart, and do not rely on your own understanding, Proverbs 3.5.

## God is God and We Are Not

> For my thoughts are not your thoughts, and your ways are not my ways. This is the LORD's declaration. For as heaven is higher than earth, so my ways are higher than your ways, and my thoughts than your thoughts, Isaiah 55.8–9.

## What Creation Reveals

Creation reminds us of and humbles us with the power of God. As we look around, we can see that someone created the world. The Psalmist says it is a silent, but awesome declaration:

> Day after day they pour out speech; night after night they communicate knowledge. There is no speech; there are no words; their voice is not heard. Their message has gone out to the whole earth, and their words to the ends of the world. In the heavens he has pitched a tent for the sun, Psalm 19.2–4.

How can anyone view creation's awesome beauty and fail to embrace the truth of an all-knowing, all-powerful, living God?

## What Scripture Reveals

When we study the authenticity, survivability, and uniqueness of God's word, we can know it is from God. Scripture is God's message to us:

> The instruction of the Lord is perfect, renewing one's life; the testimony of the Lord is trustworthy, making the inexperienced wise. The precepts of the Lord are right, making the heart glad; the command of the Lord is radiant, making the eyes light up. The fear of the Lord is pure, enduring forever; the ordinances of the Lord are reliable and altogether righteous, Psalm 19.7–9.

There are many other passages that testify to the power of what has been revealed to us: John 17.17; 2 Timothy 3.16–17; 2 Peter 1.19–21.

## This Knowledge Should Humble Us

When we experience the power and majesty of God, it reminds us that everything we have and are is due to Him. *Everything*. God is the wind beneath our wings. He is our sustainer, Psalm 55.22. He is our rock, Psalm 18.2. He is our fortress, Psalm 46.7. He is our strength, Psalm 28.7. And as His created ones, we are dependent upon Him for everything.

## God Wants Us to Live for Him

We struggle with this. Many of the passages we've just read remind us that God is awesome. Yet, He seeks to have a close, personal, and intimate relationship with each one of us. We have been created for a higher purpose for God, but we often fall short due to a lack of faith and the sin that conquers us. Sin is an indelible stain on the soul. It is the awesome, mighty God who gave His Son to die for us so that our sins would be washed away. Through that one act, God has proven for all time that He loves us. We must embrace the one who took our place, Hebrews 2.9. God has set us free and through Him we find meaning, purpose, and significance. Now, we live for Him.

> Lord, our Lord, how magnificent is your name throughout the earth!, Psalm 8.9

When we come to worship, the thought that His favor has rained down upon us should move us to profound reverence.

> I will thank the Lord with all my heart; I will declare all your wondrous works. I will rejoice and boast about you; I will sing about your name, Most High, Psalm 9.1–2

# What is Worship?

Worship is the natural response to God's amazing grace. It is in worship that God is magnified. It is in worship where our view of God is expanded. It is in worship where we are reminded of the need for humility.

> I will bless the LORD at all times; his praise will always be on my lips. I will boast in the LORD; the humble will hear and be glad. Proclaim the LORD's greatness with me; let us exalt his name together, Psalm 34.1–3.

As you read this passage, see where the focus lies. We worship in a way that brings Him glory – not us.

## Worship Happens When Your Spirit Responds to God

> Hallelujah! Give praise, servants of the LORD; praise the name of the LORD. Let the name of the LORD be blessed both now and forever. From the rising of the sun to its setting, let the name of the LORD be praised, Psalm 113.1–3.

We must worship God from the heart. Jesus mentioned this on several occasions:

- John 4.23–24—God wants our head and our heart.
- Matthew 15.8—God wants true hearts to worship Him.
- Matthew 23.23–24—A lifeless religion of obligation and routine is rejected by God. We must never replace the need to know God with a quest for knowledge about God.

The point of worship is not activity, even right activity, but intimacy with God.[58]

# God Wants Our Reverence and Passion

How do you approach worship? Are you prepared? The worship service is a special time each week where we present ourselves to God in respect and honor. It is not a social hour. It is not casual. Worship takes us to a higher level and will be seen in the way we approach God with respect.

> I rejoiced with those who said to me, "Let's go to the house of the LORD," Psalm 122.1.

God wants our passion. Can you repeat this Psalm along with David? There was emotion involved when David approached God. Worship needs to capture our heart and should be expressed in emotional ways.

---

58  Wilson Adams. Source Unknown.

# Conclusion

May God help us develop a deeper appreciation for who He is and what He has done. God wants to get below the surface and reach your heart. He wants to touch the innermost part of your being. He wants us to reach back.

# For Thought and Reflection

1. Why is it important to remind ourselves of who God is?

2. What are the two ways God reveals Himself? Are there any other ways? Explain.

3. What are some things about the creation that amaze you about God's creative power and knowledge? How does this impact you?

4. What are some things about God's revelation that humble you?

5. How do the facts concerning God's creative and revelatory power impact the way you worship? Do these things move you to greater dedication in living for Him? Explain.

6. What is worship?

7. While we can worship outside of the assembly, what is it to you that makes the Sunday worship service so special?

8. Who should be the focus on our worship assemblies? Why is this so important to keep in mind?

9. What does it mean to worship in truth? In Spirit? (John 4.23–24)

10. Should we be afraid of expressing emotion in worship? How can we guard against going to extremes on both sides of this?

Lesson 12

# The Purpose and Power of the Lord's Supper

## Introduction

Worship is an eternally important and challenging subject, and it is to be conducted in a manner to please God. It involves action on our part and is in no way associated with passiveness. When we gather, we open our heart to God and recognize His glory as the Creator. It is a time to celebrate God's grace, mercy, and forgiveness, and it is a time when we solemnly remember the price Jesus paid on the cross in the partaking of the Lord's Supper. Throughout the centuries the importance of this part of worship has been stressed. Thomas Campbell said, "New Testament worship ceases when the Lord's Supper is not observed every Lord's Day."

It is difficult to overestimate the importance and significance of the Lord's Supper.

## Understanding the Purpose of the Supper

### The Lord's Supper Is a Memorial

Jesus said, *this do in remembrance of Me*, Luke 22:19.

Paul wrote:

> For I received from the Lord what I also delivered to you, that the Lord Jesus on the night when He was betrayed took bread, and when He had given thanks, He broke it, and said, 'This is My body which is for you. Do this in remembrance of Me.' In the same way also He took the cup, after supper, saying, 'This cup is the new covenant in My blood. Do this, as often as you drink it, in remembrance of Me,'" 1 Corinthians 11:23–25.

We eat the bread in memory of His body and drink the fruit of the vine in memory of the blood He shed. It is a solemn, serious occasion where we commemorate the death of Jesus on the cross. In the moments of partaking, we relive in our minds what Jesus experienced that awful day. We can recount the agony in the garden, the sham trials put on by the Jews and Romans, the brutal whipping/beating that left Him near death, the crown of thorns driven on His head, and the intense agony He felt in every fiber of His human body while on the cross. It was the death of Jesus that made the new covenant possible. Our sins were remitted because of the blood He shed. It is important that we pause and reflect on the extreme price paid on our behalf. Sin has always required the ultimate price. In Old Testament times, those who offered sacrifices had a clear understanding that when they sinned, something had to die to make atonement for their wrongdoing. Because of our sin, Jesus had to die. He was the *Lamb of God who takes away the sins of the world,* John 1:29.

## The Lord's Supper is a Communion

Paul said:

> The cup of blessing that we bless, is it not a participation in the blood of Christ? The bread that we break, is it not a participation in the body of Christ? Because there is one bread, we who are many are one body, for we all partake of the one bread," 1 Corinthians 10:16–17.

Communion can be defined as "sharing with someone in something." In partaking of the Lord's Supper each week, we have a fresh and loving encounter with Jesus. *All believers who come to the table are the Lord's guests and He is the host.* [1] We have communion with Jesus, who is present in spirit while we partake, and we have communion with brethren of like precious faith. Christians pause together to reflect on the blessings we enjoy through Him. Think of it: because of His blood, we walk in the light (1 John 1:7), and have forgiveness of sin, 1 John 1:9. Partaking of the Supper together should remind us that we all stand equal before the cross. It is a time when we lay aside our unique backgrounds and differences so that we may unite with each other and Jesus Christ. No one comes to the cross on a better footing than someone else – we're all equal in our need for the grace of God. While partaking, we unite as one, proclaiming our thankfulness for the sacrifice. It is also a time when we pause to recognize what we share together because of Jesus' death, burial, and resurrection.

## About the Supper's Observance

### How We Partake

> Whoever, therefore, eats the bread or drinks the cup of the Lord in an unworthy manner will be guilty of profaning the body and blood of the Lord, 1 Corinthians 11:27.

Whether or not we are worthy is not under discussion in this context. By our personal righteousness, we are never worthy. When we come together for the Lord's Supper, it is to be partaken with respect for the supreme price Jesus paid for our sins. We are to eat with the understanding that it imposes certain obligations on us – to live faithfully in service to Jesus Christ. It is not a part of worship to be treated casually. Because of this, Paul wrote:

> Let a person examine himself, then, and so eat of the bread and drink of the cup. For anyone who eats and drinks without discerning the body eats and drinks judgment on himself, 1 Corinthians 11:28–29.

## Self-Examination

In 1 Corinthians 11.29, we note the need of "discerning" the body. Discern means to "recognize or comprehend mentally." The Lord's Supper was given to us to bring into clear spiritual view our Savior and His sacrifice. It is human nature to forget. As time goes by our remembrance can wane. So, each week, we come together to focus our minds on the sacrifice of Jesus. In so doing, we keep our memory clear, straight, and focused. It has been said that as we discern this action in worship, we are connected to the past, give meaning to the present, and are inspired with hope for the future. The context of 1 Corinthians 11 suggests that any thoughtless, careless participation at the Lord's Table is a failure to discern. The seriousness of the occasion cannot be overemphasized because failure to partake with reverence brings condemnation.

## A Time of Private Reflection

The Lord's Supper is an extremely private matter between the Christian and his God. This should be a time where we remember the necessity of living in a way that shows appreciation for this sacrifice. We may take His death for granted more than we would like to admit. Gathering around the table at the beginning of a new week can be like hitting the spiritual reset button, where we bring what is important back into clear focus. When we partake, it is an opportunity to reflect on whether we are truly living for Jesus. *"He died for all, that those who live might no longer live for themselves but for Him who for their sake died and was raised,"* 2 Corinthians 5:15. We should use it as an opportunity to probe into our lives:

- *Am I engaging in willful sin?*
- *Is there a sin that I am unwilling to get out in the open before God?*

- *Have I accepted His grace into my life?*

# The Power of the Lord's Supper

## We Proclaim the Lord's Death

When we partake, Christians preach a very powerful sermon:

> For as often as you eat this bread and drink the cup, you proclaim the Lord's death until He comes, 1 Corinthians 11:26.

James Burton Coffman mentions that the Lord's Supper is a *living sermon*.[2] We announce our participation in the benefits of Jesus' death. In every generation, from the first century until the Lord returns, Christians declare their belief that Jesus died for the remission of their sins. Participation in the Lord's Supper is an affirmation of our belief in the gospel of Jesus Christ. Paul wrote: "*...that Christ died for our sins in accordance with the Scriptures, that He was buried, that He was raised on the third day in accordance with the Scriptures,*" 1 Corinthians 15:3–4. We tell the world that our faith in the power of Jesus is alive and secure!

## We Declare Our Faith in His Return

Christians will partake of the Lord's Supper *until He returns*. When we eat the Supper, we look back at the death of Christ on the cross and forward to the time of His return. By partaking and looking forward to His return, we acknowledge the reality of the coming judgment on mankind. Luke recorded:

> The times of ignorance God overlooked, but now He commands all people everywhere to repent, because He has fixed a day on which He will judge the world in righteousness by a man whom He has appointed; and of this He has given assurance to all by raising Him from the dead, Acts 17:30–31.

# Conclusion

The Lord's Supper is a very special memorial of the death of Jesus Christ for our sins. It was instituted by Jesus Himself, and He expects His disciples to observe it in His memory! The first Christians were devoted in keeping its observance:

> And they devoted themselves to the apostles' teaching and fellowship, to the breaking of bread and the prayers, Acts 2:42.

The Lord's Supper is a constant, regular reminder of Jesus' sacrifice. It is a time for self-examination and re-dedication of our service to God. And it is an opportunity to build fellowship with each other inside the body of Christ. No Christian should ever lose sight of its significance.

## For Thought and Reflection

1. Define memorial.

2. What should we remember when partaking of the Lord's Supper?

3. What has the commission of sin always required?

4. Define communion.

5. When partaking of the Lord's Supper, how do we have communion with Jesus?

6. When partaking of the Lord's Supper, in what ways do we have communion with brothers and sisters in Christ?

7. Describe how one can partake of the Lord's Supper *worthily*.

8. What does it mean to *discern* the Lord's body?

9. Discuss the importance of partaking of the Lord's Supper in a serious manner.

10. What are some probing questions we can ask ourselves as we prepare to partake?

11. Was the Lord's Supper intended to be a meal designed to satisfy physical hunger?

12. What are some things we proclaim when we partake of the Lord's Supper?

## Lesson 13
# Why We Sing A Cappella

## Introduction

One of the most distinct characteristics of the churches of Christ is *a cappella* singing. Today we use that word to describe music without the use of instruments, or more simply, vocal singing. *A cappella* is an Italian word that means "in the chapel manner," i.e., human voice only.[59] That definition makes sense when we consider that for the first 1000 years of the existence of the Roman Catholic Church, only vocal music characterized the worship service. Even after the Protestant Reformation many resulting denominations continued to sing *a cappella* until the late 18th and early 19th-centuries. Across the West today, only a few churches still sing without instruments. Besides the churches of Christ, Primitive Baptists, some Amish, and Mennonite churches still have worship services characterized by *a cappella* singing.

So why do we choose to conduct our worship service this way? In this lesson we will examine the practice of the early Christians as recorded in Scripture.

## What We Learn from the New Testament

There is no clear evidence of the usage of any instrument accompanying vocal music in public worship anywhere in the New Testament.

This is remarkable when thinking of the prominence of the usage of instruments in the greater culture of the time. The gospels mention music and dancing at celebrations, Luke 15.25, flute players played in mourning ceremonies at death, Matthew 9.23, the daughter of Herodias danced before Herod, Matthew 14.6, and the children in one of Jesus' parables complained, "We played the flute for you, but you didn't dance;" Luke 7.32.[60] Paul mentioned the availability of flutes and harps in 1 Corinthians 14.7. Despite the ready availability of instruments of all sorts, the New Testament is silent regarding their usage in public worship.

---

59  Provance, Brett Scott. *Pocket Dictionary of Liturgy & Worship*. The IVP Pocket Reference Series. Downers Grove, IL: IVP Academic, 2009, p. 13.

60  Lewis, Jack P. *Basic Beliefs:* Nashville: 21st Century Christian, 2013, p. 138.

There are ten passages overall to reference. The first six passages, beginning on the night of Jesus' betrayal and then several instances in Paul's writing, show us singing was the practice of the early Christians as they gathered for corporate worship.

1. Matthew 26.30; Mark 14.26: *After **singing a hymn,** they went out to the Mount of Olives.*
2. 1 Corinthians 14.15b: *I will **sing praise** with the spirit, and I will also **sing praise** with my understanding.*
3. 1 Corinthians 14.26: *What then, brothers and sisters? Whenever you come together, **each one has a hymn**, a teaching, a revelation, a tongue, or an interpretation. Everything is to be done for building up.*
4. Ephesians 5.19: *speaking to one another in psalms, hymns, and spiritual songs, **singing and making music with your heart to the Lord** …* Note the vocal activity in the verse. We observe teaching, revelations, tongues, and interpretation. Next, we observe *speaking*. The immediate context of the verse should indicate that vocal music is in mind when Paul references *psalms, hymns, and spiritual songs*.
5. Colossians 3.16: *Let the word of Christ dwell richly among you, in all wisdom teaching and admonishing one another through psalms, hymns, and spiritual songs, **singing to God with gratitude in your hearts.*** Like the previous reference in Ephesians 5, *singing* is connected to other vocal activities: *teaching and admonishing one another*. Instrumental music does not appear to be in view.

There are five other passages which reference Christians singing:

1. Acts 16.25—Paul and Silas sang hymns while they were locked in a Philippian prison.
2. Romans 15.9—Paul quotes an Old Testament passage referencing joyous Gentiles singing praise to God for their salvation.
3. Hebrews 2.11–12—Singing that praises Jesus is also mentioned here.
4. James 5.13—those who are cheerful are directed to sing praises.

These passages lead us to conclude that instrumental music was not present in the worship of the early church. All the music mentioned in the New Testament is vocal.

# What History Reveals

Everett Ferguson, in his excellent work *A Cappella Music in the Public Worship of the Church*[61], has a comprehensive listing of statements from the early second century and beyond that provide sufficient evidence of vocal singing (and nothing else) characterizing Christian worship.

## Pliny, Roman Governor of Bithynia

During the early second century, Pliny the Younger reported to the emperor that Christians "were in the habit of meeting on a certain fixed day before it was light, **when they sang in alternate verses a hymn to Christ**, as to a god, and bound themselves by a solemn oath, not to any wicked deeds…"[62]

## Ignatius of Antioch

Ignatius of Antioch was an early second century bishop (elder) who described the unity of the church to be like what happens in worship characterized by vocal singing. "For your justly renowned presbytery, worthy of God, is fitted as exactly to the bishop as the strings are to the harp. Therefore, in your concord and harmonious love, Jesus Christ is sung. And do ye, man by man, become a choir, that being harmonious in love, and taking up the song of God in unison, **ye may with one voice sing to the Father through Jesus Christ**, so that He may both hear you, and perceive by your works that ye are indeed the members of His Son."[63] Ignatius' emphasis on "one voice," is seen throughout early Christian writings, which may find their basis in passages like Romans 15.6 where Paul emphasizes unity in the body resulting from the bringing together of many sounds.

---

61  Ferguson, Everett. *A Cappella Music in the Public Worship of the Church*. Fourth Edition. Abilene, TX: Desert Willow Publishing, 2013, p. 58.

62  Pliny. *Letters, Vols. 1 & 2*. Edited by T. E. Page, E. Capps, W. H. D. Rouse, and W. M. L. Hutchinson. Translated by William Melmoth. The Loeb Classical Library. London; New York: William Heinemann; The Macmillan Co., 1931, Plin., Ep. 10.96.

63  Ignatius of Antioch. "The Epistle of Ignatius to the Ephesians." *The Apostolic Fathers with Justin Martyr and Irenaeus*. Edited by Alexander Roberts, James Donaldson, and A. Cleveland Coxe. Vol. 1. The Ante-Nicene Fathers. Buffalo, NY: Christian Literature Company, 1885, p. 50–51.

## Justin Martyr

Justin Martyr was a Christian apologist who lived during the middle of the second century. He described and defended Christian ideals and practices. He describes Christian worship as this: "we praise to the utmost of our power by the exercise of prayer and thanksgiving for all things wherewith we are supplied, as we have been taught that the only honour that is worthy of Him is not to consume by fire what He has brought into being for our sustenance, but to use it for ourselves and those who need, **and with gratitude to Him to offer thanks by invocations and hymns for our creation**, and for all the means of health, and for the various qualities of the different kinds of things, and for the changes of the seasons; and to present before Him petitions for our existing again in incorruption through faith in Him."[64]

## Tertullian

Going into the third century, Tertullian describes Christian worship as "the reading of Scriptures, or in **the chanting of psalms**, or in the preaching of sermons, or in the offering up of prayers,"[65] In a separate writing defending love feasts to those who tried to associate it with licentiousness, Tertullian mentions that during the congregational feasts a person would be asked to "stand forth and sing, as he can, a hymn to God, either one from the holy Scriptures or one of his own composing."[66]

Ferguson also mentions how a fragment of a third century hymn has been found. The hymn contains "notations for vocal rendition but none for instrumental accompaniment."[67]

---

64  Justin Martyr. "The First Apology of Justin." *The Apostolic Fathers with Justin Martyr and Irenaeus*. Edited by Alexander Roberts, James Donaldson, and A. Cleveland Coxe. Vol. 1. The Ante-Nicene Fathers. Buffalo, NY: Christian Literature Company, 1885, p. 166.

65  Tertullian. "A Treatise on the Soul." *Latin Christianity: Its Founder, Tertullian*. Edited by Alexander Roberts, James Donaldson, and A. Cleveland Coxe, Translated by Peter Holmes. Vol. 3. The Ante-Nicene Fathers. Buffalo, NY: Christian Literature Company, 1885, p. 188.

66  Tertullian. "The Apology." *Latin Christianity: Its Founder, Tertullian*. Edited by Alexander Roberts, James Donaldson, and A. Cleveland Coxe, Translated by S. Thelwall. Vol. 3. The Ante-Nicene Fathers. Buffalo, NY: Christian Literature Company, 1885, Apol. 39, p. 47.

67  Ferguson, p. 61.

The early Christians often associated instruments with banquets and the immorality that often went along with them. Tertullian emphasized the contrast in Ephesians 5.18–19, connecting excessive drinking with instruments. He argued that in order to stay away from that, people should sing psalms and hymns.[68] A century before Tertullian, Justin Martyr also made the connection between instruments and licentiousness as he associated them with pagan religious practices: "There are excessive banquetings, and subtle flutes which provoke to lustful movements, and useless and luxurious anointings, and crowning with garlands."[69] In these writings the vocal music of hymns by Christians was held up by the church fathers in contrast. One writer says, "Let us take up hymns instead of timbrels, psalmody instead of lewd dances and songs, thankful acclamation instead of theatrical clapping …"[70]

## Eusebius

At the beginning of the fourth century the historian Eusebius wrote a commentary on Psalm 65.10–15. Ferguson provides the quote: "Throughout the world—in cities, in villages, and in the country—in all the churches of God the people of Christ, who have been chosen out of all the nations, send up, not to the native gods nor to demons but to the one God spoken of by the prophets, **hymns and psalmody with a loud voice so that the sound of those singing can be heard by those standing outside.**"[71]

There is a great deal more of historical evidence out there which proves an absence of any instrumental music in the church for at least the first millennium after Christ. The choice of the early Christians to sing was

---

68   Tertullian writes: "The command, to "sing to the Lord with psalms and hymns,"(Ephesians 5.19) comes suitably from him who knew that those who "drank wine with drums and psalteries" (Isaiah 5.11–12) were blamed by God." Tertullian. "The Five Books against Marcion." *Latin Christianity: Its Founder, Tertullian*. Edited by Alexander Roberts, James Donaldson, and A. Cleveland Coxe, Translated by Peter Holmes. Vol. 3. The Ante-Nicene Fathers. Buffalo, NY: Christian Literature Company, 1885, Adv. Marc. 5.18, p. 468.

69   Justin Martyr. "The Discourse to the Greeks." *The Apostolic Fathers with Justin Martyr and Irenaeus*. Edited by Alexander Roberts, James Donaldson, and A. Cleveland Coxe, Translated by M. Dods. Vol. 1. The Ante-Nicene Fathers. Buffalo, NY: Christian Literature Company, 1885, p. 272.

70   Ferguson, p. 91.

71   Ferguson, p. 62.

intentional. Some believe the organ did not come into the Catholic church until the tenth or eleventh century, and even then, it was a separate part of the worship service and did not replace the existing style of music. The Eastern churches today mostly still sing *a cappella.*

As the Reformation came, many of the Reformed and Anabaptist churches rejected instrumental music as they associated it with Catholicism. Zwingli and Calvin were both opposed to instrumental music, and its reintroduction in the 18th and 19th centuries was met with great opposition.

I will close this section with a quote from Ferguson:

> *A cappella* comes from the Latin by way of Italian and is used to mean "in the style of the church," "as is done in the church." The classical form of church music is unaccompanied song. To abstain from the use of the instrument is not a peculiar aberration of "a frontier American sect": this was easily, until comparatively recent times, the majority tradition of Christian history. Virtually no one has said it is wrong to worship *a cappella*, whereas many have thought instrumental music in worship is wrong. It may not appear to be true today, but against the whole sweep of Christian history *a cappella* music is the truly ecumenical ground to occupy.[72]

## Why We Sing

History is good to know, but our reasons for abstaining from instrumental music in public worship go much farther, i.e., our relationship with God. Our primary desire is to *please God in worship.* This was a major theme of the New Testament writers as seen in 2 Corinthians 5.9; Ephesians 5.8–10; Colossians 1.9–10; 1 Thessalonians 4.1–2; 1 John 3.21–22; Hebrews 13.15–16; and 1 Timothy 2.1–3. Pleasing God was foremost in their mind!

When we come together to worship, what we offer should be an expression of each individual's personal relationship with God. One of the functions of that assembly is praise, where we, in unison with other believers, offer our best to God. It is not about what pleases us or what sounds good. Emotion is very much a part of worship and parts of it may be very appealing, but those are all products of something higher ... i.e., our very personal connection with God where our hearts are joined with His in spiritual worship. The objective of worship is not to get an emotional high or feeling of euphoria, the objective is to exalt God and reverence Him. The natural result of that will bear itself out in our emotions of joy, thankfulness, and gratitude. One

---

72   Ferguson, p. 98.

aim sets out to please oneself ... the other sets out to please God. Just because something pleases us does not mean it pleases God.

Lewis aptly illustrates the proper aim of worship:

> If I am going to give my wife a present, I am not likely to give her something because I like it or want it. I would not get her a set of golf clubs, a circular saw, or a new computer. I would find something she wants. If I am going to offer something to God, and I want him to be pleased with it, I have to offer what He has specified He wants. Singing has been specified. Instrumental music has not been specified.[73]

If we are to know what pleases God, we must look to Scripture:

> Additionally then, brothers and sisters, we ask and encourage you in the Lord Jesus, that as you have received instruction from us on how you should live and please God—as you are doing—do this even more. For you know what commands we gave you through the Lord Jesus, 1 Thessalonians 4.1–2.

## What Has God Specified?

So, what does the word indicate as to what pleases God in worship? The Hebrew writer, I believe, has put it succinctly:

> Therefore, through him let us continually offer up to God a sacrifice of praise, that is, the fruit of lips that confess his name. Don't neglect to do what is good and to share, for God is pleased with such sacrifices, Hebrews 13.15–16.

True worship consists of the praise of God (13.15), and the shared life of love (13.16). Now, let's connect something Paul said in 1 Corinthians:

> What then? I will pray with the spirit, and I will also pray with my understanding. I will sing praise with the spirit, and I will also sing praise with my understanding, 1 Corinthians 14.15.

Praise of God is expressed through our prayers and singing. This is backed up by the references we looked at in the beginning of the lesson where *singing* is mentioned in reference to corporate or public worship.

Nowhere in the New Testament has God indicated that He is pleased with adding instruments into the public worship service. It is true that God has not specifically said, "Thou shalt not use instrumental music in worship." However, to indicate His expectations, God is not required to list out everything offered in worship that He does not desire. We couldn't get through the list if He did.

---

73   Lewis, p. 140.

It is because of this; we choose to refrain. Not because we are anti-music, but because our primary aim is to please God. "All Christians will agree that God will receive all the glory that He intends to give Him by singing without an instrument." All should agree that "we can make all the melody God wants us to make in the heart as the designated instrument to accompany our songs. Let us make a joyful noise to the Lord and sing with grace in our hearts to God."[74]

## For Thought and Reflection

1. How prominent were instruments in first century culture? How does this emphasize the significance of the absence of instrumental music in the public worship of the early church?

2. What did Ignatius say regarding the practice of music in the second century church?

3. What do you think about the early Christians making the association of instruments with banqueting and immorality, while comparing that to the singing of Christians to worship God?

4. As you read some of the history listed in this lesson, does it appear the choice made to sing without instruments was intentional?

---

74  Wharton, p. 160.

5. What should be our primary desire in public worship?

6. Is *emotion* the aim? Or is emotion *the result* of a higher aim in public worship? Explain.

7. How can we know what pleases God?

8. Is God required to explain or specify everything that does not please Him? Explain.

9. If we are committed to restoring the church of the New Testament, upon what could we agree regarding the music of the early church?

10. Why do you think this issue has been so divisive inside the Restoration Movement?

www.ingramcontent.com/pod-product-compliance
Lightning Source LLC
Chambersburg PA
CBHW040322050426
42453CB00017B/2434